# Net
# Know-How

### *Surviving the Bloodbath—*
### Straight Talk from
### 25 Internet Entrepreneurs

by
**Jim Romeo**

Aegis Publishing Group, Ltd.
796 Aquidneck Avenue
Newport, Rhode Island
401-849-4200
*www.aegisbooks.com*

Aegis Publishing Group, Ltd.
796 Aquidneck Avenue
Newport, RI  02842

International Standard Book Number: 1-890154-24-5

Printed in the United States of America.

10 9 8 7 6 5 4 3 2 1

R01785l6018

*For Jeannie, James, and Danielle —*

*you light up my life.*

# Acknowledgments

IT'S BEEN A LONG HAUL! Theodore Roosevelt once said that he was the "most un-Harvard-like man to go to Harvard." I suppose it could be said that I was the most "unpublishable-like" person to ever get published.

It all started with my own wager to make back the $25 I spent on a *Writer's Market* book. Over 300 articles in hundreds of publications later, I just can't believe I've done it!

For her encouragement all along the way, I need to thank my wife Jeannie, who always tolerated me opening the mail before I ate dinner and always supported me in my crazy interests and behavior .

I also must thank my publisher, Bob Mastin of Aegis Publishing Group, who gave me the opportunity to be a published author. After three agents and numerous replies from publishers who would hardly give me the time of day, it was truly refreshing to meet Bob and develop this book for him.

To the numerous entrepreneurs in this book who took the time to respond and pour out their innermost thoughts—I am grateful. It was harder than I thought to get people to speak to me, but I have gained a newfound respect for the courage and hardened guts that an entrepreneur has to have.

So, to the guys and girls who did it and are doing it (while most of us only dream about it)—my hat's off to all of you and the bravery that you exemplify!

And last, but certainly not least, I must thank the Lord, my God, from Whom all good things come. If it were not for His inspiration, will, guidance, and wisdom, I never could have pulled this or anything else off.

— Jim Romeo

# Table of Contents

INTRODUCTION .......................................................... 13

## PROFILES

AbleTV.net ................................................ 17
About.com ................................................ 27
ask dr. tech ............................................. 39
AskJeeves.com ........................................... 45
Blink.com ................................................ 55
BookZone.com ........................................... 63
Business Know-How ................................... 73
CarePackages.com ..................................... 79
Collages.net ............................................ 87
Culturefinder.org ..................................... 95
Developer's Network ................................. 103
eHealthInsurance.com ............................... 109
eMarketer.com ......................................... 121
E-Poll.com .............................................. 131
Experience.com ....................................... 141
FeedRoom.com ......................................... 151
MeTV.com ............................................... 157
Mile High Comics ..................................... 169

<u>PROFILES</u> (continued)

Multicity.com ....................................................... 175
Oingo.com ........................................................... 183
RightNow.com ..................................................... 191
seeUthere.com ..................................................... 197
Tyler-Adam.com ................................................... 209
WantedTechnologies ........................................... 215
Winebid.com ...................................................... 221

MARKETING TIPS ........................................................ 227

TIPS FROM KEVIN NUNLEY ...................................... 235

BUILD A BETTER WEBSITE ........................................ 265

A FEW LAST WORDS ................................................... 269

APPENDIX ..................................................................... 271

# Introduction

· · · · · · · · · · · · · · · · · · · · · · · · · · · · · · · · · · · · · ·

WHILE PUTTING TOGETHER this book, I couldn't help but think of Billy Joel's song, "The Piano Man." In it he sings, "John at the bar is a friend of mine, who gives me my drinks for free. He's quick with a joke or a light of your smoke, but there's someplace that he'd rather be."

Do you remember it? Some of you may not be old enough to remember, but Billy Joel later goes on to quote this guy John as saying, "I'm sure that I could be a movie star, if I could get out of this place."

Well, there's a little bit of John in most of us, and there's a lot of John in the 25 persons profiled in this book. All 25 of them went out to pursue their dreams. There was someplace that they'd rather be! Like John in Billy Joel's song, the 25 persons profiled all seem to have had that same passion. They were sure that they could be a movie star in their own right—their own right being a business of their own somewhere in cyberspace.

Eugene Carr, the founder of Culturefinder.com, had told me that a year in dot-com life is equal to ten years anywhere else. So, as I worked on this book, I worried that these 25 would go belly up by the time I was ready to go to press.

It is quite likely that some of those profiled in this book won't always be a going concern. The Internet start-up frenzy isn't what it used to be, and new entrants are in decline. But before you conclude that the dot-com bubble has burst once and for all, wait a bit. The Internet isn't dead.

The things that do seem to be in decline are the parties, the razor scooters, the raspberry mineral water, the oxygen tents, the in-house massage therapists, and all the funky Internet-cool perks that seem to characterize a dot-com on its way down the drain. It's looks like Jeff Pledger, the founder of AbleTV.net, is right when he says the dot-coms are returning to traditional economics. So what can you learn from start-up stories?

The 25 stories herein are full of valuable lessons that would take a lot of time and effort to discover on your own. There are rare insights that can be learned from each story. Indeed, there's always much to be learned from any start-up story. What matters most is the thinking pattern of each entrepreneur.

Had this book been written in the midst of the industrial revolution—profiling Andrew Carnegie, Henry Frick, the Vanderbilts, the Kennedys, the Mellons, and the Rockefellers—I'm sure you'd discover some common elements in the thought patterns of these entrepreneurs. The same is true today.

While attending Columbia University's Graduate School of Business, I recall that Peters and Waterman's *In Search Of Excellence* was required reading for my Management of Organizations class. This book profiled those companies the authors found to be excellent and examined how they were managed. But even these outstanding companies didn't all survive. Several of the companies featured in the book later went out of business or were swallowed up by larger conglomerates. Nonetheless, my last check in a bookstore showed that *In Search of Excellence* was still for sale. And that's my point.

The "how" of a company seems to be more valuable information than "whatever became of it?" It's inspiring to read how these companies were created, regardless of when it took place or who the characters were. I suppose this is because the path entrepreneurs take to get up and off the ground is one of the hardest things to understand when you're trying to pursue your own gig. It's where we most need a map, mentor, or template to show us how it's done.

You just can't tell me that reading about some of these stories isn't fascinating—or even way cool:

- Jennifer Floren, who started Experience.com while only in her twenties.

- Benjamin Mark, who read about designing a Web page and stumbled onto a few new customers with his website—all while operating a jewelry business in midtown Manhattan.

- Jeff Pledger, who is blind, founded AbleTV.net, which now serves a global community of persons with disabilities.

- Ryan Moran, who used to muse with his brother and friends around a campfire about this concept of sending care packages to our loved ones.

- Ari Paparo, who pursued a business start-up in lieu of a fast-track MBA career path.

And there are more—20 more in fact.

Each story offers something helpful, and there's at least one little spark of valuable information presented by each company pro-filed in this book. You know, it only takes one spark to light a flame. And that flame just might give enough light to those of us who feel the same way as John in Billy Joel's "The Piano Man"—there's someplace that we'd rather be.

*I try to get
people to see what I have.
When you run a computer company,
you have to get people
to buy into your dreams.*

*— Steve Jobs*

# 1

# AbleTV.net

. . . . . . . . . . . . . . . . . . . . . . . . . . . . . . . . . . . .

### *A global TV network*
### *for persons with disabilities*

YOU'VE HEARD IT SO MANY times before—the Web has changed our lives. But an often unsung topic of the digital frontier is what it has done for the 54 million disabled persons around the globe. Digital technology has enabled persons with all types of disabilities to gain access to worlds that may have been otherwise unavailable to them. Through sites such as AbleTV.net, access is now possible.

Jeff Pledger, who lost his eyesight at age 27, started AbleTV.net to serve this market. His website serves business, consumers, and government with multimedia that is accessible by persons with a wide range of disabilities. Listen to Jeff Pledger, and you'll get a heartening dose of what this unique business is all about.

**Can you tell us about your firm and what one finds when they visit your site?**

AbleTV provides TV the way you need it. We are the first global TV network for people with disabilities, powered by accessibility via the Web. When you visit our website at www.abletv.net, you will find a wide array of accessible video content that is available for viewing 24 hours a days, 365 days a year. These videos cover a wide variety of topics, including video product demonstrations of helpful technology to social activities. However, all of the videos have a common theme. They all work toward making things accessible for people with disabilities.

When you come to our website, you will find the largest collection of accessible videos that can be viewed on the Web. You are probably wondering what I mean by "accessible" video content? Good question. The problem with showing videos over the Web is that it takes for granted that you have all of your faculties available to watch and enjoy the content. This isn't necessarily the case for people with disabilities.

If you are deaf or hard of hearing, you don't have access to the audio output, so there is a need for captioning on the videos. If you are blind or visually impaired, you don't get the meaning being brought out in the video segments that are strictly visual. Therefore, there is the need for audio description of the action.

For those who are learning or cognitively impaired, the redundancy of output with both captioning and audio descriptions will reinforce the meaning of the content. These accessible solutions take advantage of concepts known as "universal design principles" (UDP), which allow the content to reach broader market segments, but at lower marginal costs.

These accessible solutions aren't just for people with disabilities, but can be applied to any number of situations. If you can't play a video with audio output, for whatever reason, the captioning provides a means for understanding the content. Again, if you can't keep your visual attention to the video, for whatever reason, the audio descriptions provide the means for understanding the content.

***Tell us a little about yourself and how you came to found this business?***

I lost my sight at age 27 due to illness. I was employed by Bell Atlantic as a senior systems specialist and database manager for nine years and represented Bell Atlantic on the Disabled Access Committee on X-Windows (DACX) and the Telecommunications Access Advisory Committee for Section 255 of the Telecommunications Act (TAAC). I also appeared as a guest panelist on the President's Committee for the Employment of People with Disabilities.

In addition, while at Bell Atlantic, I coauthored a patent for a process to mechanize telephone dialing through voice recognition. I should also mention that I'm an avid runner and have completed 12 marathons, including New York, Boston, Rome, and Poland. Currently I compete through the Achilles Track Club for disabled athletes, and since 1989, I have been the American blind record holder for a super marathon (62 miles/100K).

*Can you tell us what a typical day is like for you? What sort of technology do you use at your workstation?*

I travel to work via the mass transit system here in the greater Washington DC area. I do this with my companion, Oliver, a black Labrador retriever who has been my guide dog for the past 8 years and is the CCO (chief canine officer) of AbleTV, Inc. He is a good match for me, as he truly loves to work as I do.

As for the assistive technology that I use to access my workstation, my solutions are fairly straightforward. I use a screen reading application that allows me to interact with the Windows GUI (graphical user interface). I have several different voice synthesizers that I take advantage of for various reasons, depending upon whether I need to use a desktop or laptop computer, for example. I do have a Braille printer, which I use to make hard copies of material I might need for a meeting or other scenarios, but I use it only when needing a hard copy.

A very important part of my work environment is the scanner and OCR (optical character recognition) software I use to process printed material. My scanner also has an ADF(automatic document feeder), which can hold up to 50 pages—very convenient for putting the pages on the scanner. I just click the auto process button, walk away and get a cup of coffee, then come back to turn the pages over and process the backs of the pages, and let the software collate the pages in proper order so that I can read them effectively.

At the end of the day, Oliver gets me home safe and sound to my family—my wife, Suzanne, and my daughter, Caroline. I try my best to spend quality time with them, so it is usually late at night that I will resume work on beta testing software and hardware products for people with disabilities. A long day, but rewarding.

*How did the firm and its site come to be? Is there an interesting story behind your start-up?*

I think there is a very interesting story behind how we got started. My wife, Suzanne, used to work for a computer wholesale distributor in Reston, Virginia. I would pick up my daughter, Caroline, after I got out of work and then meet Suzanne in Reston so that we could travel home together as a family.

On one particular occasion, I was waiting for Suzanne in a local restaurant (Caroline wasn't with me that day), enjoying a good beer and an equally good cigar. However, my cigar went out and I was out of matches, so I went looking for a light. I ran into Dave Gardy, then CEO of TVontheWEB, a video-streaming provider.

We got to talking about our respective jobs and Dave wondered how a blind person could interact within the graphical Windows environment. So, I took out my laptop and connected the voice synthesizer and gave him a brief demonstration of how a screen reader gives you the information that is displayed within a given Windows application.

A few more beers and cigars later, we got to talking about video streaming and related issues as I saw them from an accessibility standpoint. Dave, being a business person, wasn't too impressed until we started talking about the size of the market segment consisting of people with disabilities.

I informed him that approximately 20 percent of the American population have a disability, and that number is increasing on a daily basis. This 20 percent equaled about 49 million people at the time (1997) and grew to an estimated 54 million Americans in 2000. And that was just the domestic number—the world-wide number is estimated to be somewhere in the vicinity of 750 million people. Dave became impressed and interested. More beers and cigar smoking.

It was about this time that my wife got off work and found us having just a real good old time. She joined us, and we started brainstorming for a name for the company. We went around the table numerous times, all in vain, trying to come up with something that would work. Suzanne ordered an appetizer of chicken wings, then suddenly looked at us and said, "What about AbleTV?" Excitement went around the table as this was truly the right name for the company. The rest of the story is history.

### Where, when, and how did you come up with the idea for your business?

I guess the idea was always there, but the it was lacking a mechanism to drive it. I have been involved in what I call assistive technology for the past 14 years or so, and I have been going to numerous conferences dealing specifically with this technology. What I found over the years is that generally the same people come to the same conferences year in and year out. This is due to the availability of resources, money, time, etc. Don't get me wrong, there are new faces each year, but many of the same ones come back year after year.

The locations of these conferences are restricted to the number of people that can attend and the availability of hotel rooms and other accommodations. OK, let's play some number games. Let's say that there are 24 conferences around the U.S. dealing specifically with assistive technologies and people with disabilities. This number maybe low or high, it doesn't matter, it is just a number.

Now let's say that the hotel(s) where the conference is taking place can hold approximately 4,000 people with disabilities. That is a fair number, so let's just use that as a standard. Now let's go even further and say that these 4,000 people with disabilities go to one of the 24 conferences, so that there is no duplication in attendance. I think they call this "mutually exclusive" from a statistical standpoint. So, 24 conferences each with 4,000 attendees equals 96,000 people with disabilities going to these conferences and gaining the information from them.

Here's the clincher. What's the probability that 96,000 people with disabilities will have the opportunity and the ability to reach the remaining 53 million or so individuals with disabilities in America? Slim to none.

Trying to convince broadcast network TV to cover these conferences is tough—it might make the nightly news for about 60 seconds, but that's it. The Web is the natural and most cost-effective way to reach this market segment.

**Can you tell us about some of your customers? Are they individuals? Businesses? Where are they from and what do they order?**

What we do is create accessible solutions for consumers, businesses and the government. To date we've had corporate customers and consumers. We're just getting ready to move into the government arena.

We provide the ability to disseminate information in a format that's accessible for people using universal design principles. That is creating the opportunity to reach the largest market segment at the lowest marginal cost.

So if I have a plain old video, you can see it and you can hear it. But if you're deaf or hard of hearing, it does you no good. If you're blind or have low vision, it certainly does you no good. If you have a learning or cognitive impairment, it does you no good. If you have any mental health illness, it does you no good. If you're a busy person, it does you no good.

But now let's add captioning to the video. The captioning is searchable. So now you've got a reference point to be able to look at things. If we add audio description to the video, it now gives benefits to those who can't see. The combination of both the audio and the description enhances the beauty of the medium for even people without disabilities.

There's a video up on our website showing a performance of the Infinity Dance Troop. It's a ballet by people with and without disabilities. If you understand dance, you can interpret what they're doing. But most people don't have that knowledge base, so we had it audio-described by a choreographer who gave a meaningful interpretation to what was going on.

### Looking back, what were some of the biggest obstacles facing the company in getting off the ground?

The traditional things that any company has to deal with. One is defining the market. It's one thing to say there are 54 million Americans with disabilities. So, you say OK, fine—how many of them have access to the Internet? You begin paring down your numbers and it certainly is a definable market.

I estimate the market to be between 3.5 to 5 million people domestically who have access to the Internet. Now some people say that's a lot less than 54 million, and it is, but I think 3.5 million people is a worthwhile market.

Look at it worldwide and it gets bigger. That was the biggest obstacle in selling the idea that, yes, there is a viable market out there.

There's also the understanding of what it takes to run a business. The understanding of what the real costs are of running a business. I did such and such today. How much money did I make? Was it worth my day getting up out of bed? These are the things you look at and say, "I need to accomplish steps one, two, and three today so I can move to steps four, five, and six."

After that, I guess the hardest thing was being able to get our first sponsorship from Microsoft. That was really a big boost for us. That gave us, number one, instant credibility, and it looked to give us the seed money to get us started and up off the ground.

The toughest thing, though, the thing that we're still grappling with is finishing up our business plan. God knows you need that if you want to get outside investment.

That's the thing that really kills you. You're running the business. You're bootstrapping. You're trying to make ends meet. And then you're trying to come home after a long hard day and say, "All right, now I'm going to spend four hours writing a business plan tonight."

I have to be able to be creative. I have to be able to write convincing prose that's going to sway someone to say, "OK, I'm gonna give you half a million dollars."

You have to have passion for what you do. If you're just looking to make a lot of money and get out—I think those days are over.

**With the benefit of hindsight, how would you advise someone else to get such a business off the ground?**

Sit down and truly organize your thoughts. And if you have to, make sure that it makes sense to you. And give it to someone else—like your mother. Make it pass the mom test! If you can make it pass the mom test, it will work!

You've got to have a definite structure. Even if you're bootstrapping, you've got to have definite structure.

**Often business ventures are inspired by great leaders and other business start-up stories. Are there any inspirational leaders, books, or other business ventures that served as an inspirational model to your business?**

*Thriving on Chaos* by Tom Peters is one book that I really liked. I also like the Guy Kawasaki story from Garage.com. Steven Jobs was certainly an inspiration, also. I can run down the list of business people, but it also goes to other things.

There's a runner from San Francisco, Harry Cordello, who was blind. Back in the '70s, he was probably running 2:30 marathons. By far, one of the best, completely blind runners in the country before they started having organizations to judge him. Some of the things that he did in the face of adversity were inspirational. People who aren't afraid to take the bull by the horns are the most inspiring to me.

**Looking down the road, where is the Internet going? In light of this, where is your site going?**

I think the Internet is going to shake out. I actually think the dot-com frenzy is going to pan out and what is going to happen is that investors will be going back to basic economics. Showing me a business plan on a napkin is no longer going to work.

It will be more like, "OK, that's a great idea, but how are you going to make money?" Show me how you make money. It's the bricks-and-mortar type of idea, and being able to put a new spin on it, that's going to make it fly out into the cyber world.

We live in a capitalistic society, and a capitalistic society runs by the model of revenue and cost. If you lose sight of that, you're doomed to go out of business.

I think we're (AbleTV.net) progressing forward, while we're bootstrapping and making some tough decisions. I foresee us as being one of the industry leaders for video streaming accessible multimedia content that's on the Web. I also see us as filling a void out there on the Internet. We're looking to meet the requirements of people, businesses, and the government.

# 2

# About.com

The site that actually tried to squeeze the whole
universe onto the Internet—and pretty well succeeded

IT'S SAFE TO SAY THAT at About.com, there's something for
everyone. It doesn't look or feel like a "site," but rather like a
conglomerate of channels covering most every interest you can
imagine.

You can find the rules of cribbage, crock pot recipes, word
puzzles, parenting advice, and 696 more channels. Each channel is led by a "guide." Guides are knowledgeable about their
particular topics and can lead you through articles and links
about the subject you've chosen. Hence the name: About.com.

The site was founded by Scott Kurnit, a man known to many
dot-com aficionados as enterprising, persistent, and downright
shrewd. Kurnit began the venture as The Mining Company,
which touted itself as being visited each month by one in five of
all online users. It also laid claim to being the seventh most
visited site on the Net.

Kurnit is a remarkable person with a great story, and we grabbed
the opportunity to speak to Scott about the business of dot-
com.

**Could you tell us a little bit about how your firm came to
be and how the concept came about?**

I started the company in '96. Immediately before this I had been running the joint venture of MCI and Newscorp, which was a large Internet business built on a model that Newscorp had started. MCI, where I was working, invested in the enterprise, which resulted in a large number of people under one roof, creating a very large Internet content service.

It became clear to me that the existing organizational structure didn't take advantage of the power of the Net. The About Guide is really the cornerstone of About.com, and we have now received several patents for this model of a distributed work force.

When creating this service, we found we could get a high-quality person to operate more efficiently if we could build all the tools the Internet relied on to link people together. The outgrowth of this was to use the same model for distribution. By having large numbers of distribution partners, we'd reduce our overall cost of distribution.

At the beginning the question was, how do you produce something that's going to eventually be very large, yet do it with relatively low start-up capital, in what, at the time, was a somewhat soft financing market? And how do you get your business out there before a lot of other guys realize that the Internet's for real?

**Was this your own idea or was it a collaboration of ideas with others?**

It is something that I wanted to do when I was at Prodigy. Bill Day, who is our president and chief operating officer, worked for me at Prodigy. And while we weren't specifically discussing the details of this structure, elements of what we do were the kinds of things of things that Bill and I kicked around.

I wanted to do it again at MCI, where part of our business plan was something we called the "Internet Co-op." But the other issues of the company, in terms of access and content for Newscorp properties, took precedence. So I was able to secure some financing, and as soon as I had the first financing in place, I called Bill and said, "What I want to do is a lot of what we've talked about before, so let's develop it."

*You use the concept of guides to direct visitors to sites that suit their interests. Was that something you thought of on your own or did you, you know, adopt it from any other trend of thought?*

At the very beginning, we actually contemplated a franchise structure, where entities would buy slots on the network and then produce content areas in a consistent-looking field. We adjusted that to the guide model, which consists of independent contractors operating company-owned sites, so that we would have greater control over the total experience.

The problem with franchising is that each franchisee carries too much weight. In something that moves as quickly as the Net, we figured we'd get ourselves into a lot of trouble if we had franchisees who could go in different directions.

We looked at the franchise model, and we looked at the network TV model on two levels—product acquisition and distribution. Because I come out of television, I understand the network TV model. There is the product acquisition and creative side of network television, which historically has not owned its content, although networks have started to be much more aggressive about owning content recently. Then there is the distribution side, where broadcasters didn't own the majority of their stations. They owned 25 percent a few years ago and are now up to 30-plus percent of the stations.

We asked ourselves, how can we create a structure where we can control our distribution and content creation more vigorously than network television? Network television is good because it reaches across a wide segment of the audience. But we'd like to have control over distribution and content creation too, which is inherent in our model.

And second, if network television doesn't create targeted marketing opportunities nearly as well as cable channels, how can we take advantage of that? Because I come out of the cable business as well as network television, I appreciated the importance of targeted marketing using our 700 vertical categories, which are really the equivalent of 700 cable TV channels.

*Today your site enjoys lots of traffic. I understand it's the seventh most-visited site! What do you feel drives people there? How does one hear about it and go there?*

One, we have very good word of mouth working for us, which is obviously the best kind of marketing because it doesn't cost anything.

Number two, we have good listings throughout the Internet on people's websites and search engines, and these drive people back to our core site.

Three, we have very good customer loyalty. People who come and use us tend to come back again.

So we've addressed the three main categories that don't cost money, and if you can market a product without spending money, you've obviously got a very special opportunity. We take that very seriously as one of the core benefits of the company.

Additionally, we do spend money on affiliate deals, and we have historically spent money on big distribution deals. But recently we have been able to grow the business quite organically by traffic that comes to us for free from search engine placements, from word of mouth, and from loyal customers who just keep coming back, which is obviously the best way to run a business.

**You're located in New York, and many dot-com companies are located in Northern California and Silicon Valley. Do you feel that makes any difference at all?**

Yes, I think there's a benefit to being in New York, and we chose not only to be in New York, but to be in midtown. While a lot of companies headed for the lower end of Manhattan, we seriously felt that this was going to very quickly grow into an industry, and not just a boutique business like those in "Silicon Alley."

By the way, that is a term I personally can't stand because it sounds like a small, narrow offshoot of Silicon Valley. New York is the media capital of the world, and we are currently located a block from the U.N. We are running sites now out of 20 different countries, and we think it is very important to have an international presence.

There is a strong, but different, kind of competition for workers in New York than there is in the Valley. We are able to attract people out of traditional media companies because this is an area where we excel. So I think that recruiting has probably been easier here than in the Valley. Also, New York is the center of the advertising world, so the revenues that are largely powering the Net tend to originate from this relatively small island we've made our home.

**What would you say were some of the biggest obstacles facing you and this company in getting off the ground?**

Financing—no question about it. Particularly in the very early days when the concept was considered by many to be too grand and too unknown. It was tough to point to other models. And there was the issue of distributor work force and the issue of the quality of guidance from independent contractors. Can you get them? Will they be good if you get them? Will they stay, even if they're good? And then, how do we know that it all rolls up to being a high-quality service?

In the early stages of financing the business, I learned a lesson. Sometimes the businesses that are toughest to fund give you the best opportunities because you have to work harder at them. You have to develop distribution techniques and efficiencies in your business that you probably wouldn't have to develop if you have plenty of financial resources.

I remember talking to Scott Cook, who started Intuit. He said that his biggest piece of luck was that he couldn't get anybody to finance the business in the early days. This meant that he had to finance it all by himself, which meant he ended up owning a lot more of the business. In a lot of ways, I think you have a better business when your core staff are the real believers who are struggling to make it work.

***Well, let's pose this as a second part to the last question. If you were going to advise a couple of entrepreneurs, or "wannabe" entrepreneurs, who haven't had the experience you had before launching your business, what advice would you give them?***

First and foremost, take more money at each round of financing than you think you need. It's always easier to get additional money when you have plenty of money in the bank. I think this is a standard entrepreneurial error, because you assume you will create more value with a certain amount of dollars than you actually do.

As with anything else in life, you're going to have to jump over hurdles you didn't expect along the way. On the financial side, that means that you're going to deplete some cash. So, that's probably the most important advice.

Next, if you're in the Internet, make sure your business model uses the very fabric of the Net. We've seen business models or businesses that have not done well, even after going public. When we compare those models with our own, the difference is that we are deeply woven into the Net at the production, distribution, and modernization levels—the three legs of any business.

There are just too many businesses that don't rely on the efficiencies in the medium itself to produce and distribute. And those that do are going to do better than those that are more conventional.

For example, we see traditional media companies using television air time to try and drive traffic to the Web. That's not nearly as efficient as having a product that is completely integrated into the Net, such as we've been able to accomplish.

So, an entrepreneur who doesn't have the advantages of free media—and this is true for any business—must be fully ingrained in that business. Know the customers. Know the competitors inside out. Know the medium in which you are operating, and take advantage of whatever efficiencies you can find in it.

***Was there a point where you looked at the business and said, "This is working. I see it. It's going to fly."***

I actually thought that from the very beginning. I will confess that there were many people in the financial community and the venture capital community who didn't agree with me. Yet, even when I came back from a series of unproductive meetings, I was never deterred. Even when reaching into my own pocket to cover payroll a couple of times, I always believed.

At the same time, it was always a little disconcerting that some of the best minds in both the business and the venture capital community didn't agree with me. And you know, in looking back, I probably should have said, "Hey, if so-and-so and so-and-so don't think this is a good idea, maybe I should get out and go get myself a regular job." But, to be perfectly honest, either because I convinced myself or just always knew, I never wavered.

And I think that's an important lesson for other entrepreneurs. You know your business better than anyone else, especially those guys who give you only a couple of hours to explain it to them. If you're confident in it, go with your instincts. I believe there are a lot of businesses that should have seen the light of day but didn't because of things like that.

**You hear about a lot of businesses that will "take time" to succeed. How much time? Do you think there's a certain minimum amount of time needed to succeed in this sort of business?**

It took us three years from inception to become a public company. Today, there are companies that can do it in far less time because they have learned from those who have gone before. In some cases, going public is no end game. It is no demonstration of success, because you literally make your success every day.

I think that different companies must have a different benchmark as to what success is. It is easier today to build more capability—I won't say value, but more functionality and capability—in less time than it was yesterday because you learn from other people, the tools get better, and access is improved. So, that's a benefit.

But the downside is that as each day goes by, it is tougher to penetrate the market and get the attention of your potential customer base. It's an interesting trade-off there.

Now, all that said, there's still enormous untapped opportunity in this medium. At best, we are still at the top of the second or third inning in what is still an incredibly dynamic game. So, for entrepreneurs with great ideas and capabilities, the market is wide open in my opinion.

**Many entrepreneurs and successful business leaders have had somebody or something that's really inspired them.**

***Is there any particular leader or manager or book or figure that has acted as tremendous inspiration to you?***

Yes, actually a couple. I would have to start with my dad, who ran his own business. I had the good fortune of growing up with dinner table conversation about work, and I was well aware that he was making less than guys who worked for him. So, it didn't pain me for the year and a half where I made nothing and everybody else was making something.

Those were great lessons—the hard work and long hours that were required to run a business. If I wanted to see my dad, I had to go to the office on Saturdays or Sundays to be there with him. I had the added good fortune to be the third of three, so I actually saw more of him than my other two brothers, but I learned from their stories.

Then there was Steve Ross, who ran Warner Communications when I worked there. He was one of the great executives of our time in terms of management focus on the company and providing an environment where people felt so special, they gave 110 percent all the time. As a leader, he had an amazing capacity to foster that attitude throughout the entire organization.

And there was Steve Case, who I watched from afar in the early days when I was at Prodigy. This is a guy who is driven. He created a successful business model, and he would walk through walls to get it done. He knew all the ins and outs, and he was there during the times they had tough going. But through force of will and a really strong management team, he was able to pull it out.

Several others along the way have taught me things about negotiating, such as Tony Cox, who I worked for at Showtime, and Sheldon Terry, who I worked for at Warner. Each of these guys have very different kinds of negotiating skills and business skills, and I learned from both.

So, I think I've been fortunate. I believe I'm the average age of a public company Internet CEO—actually quite old at 46. But, in reality, that is the average age. I was lucky to have worked at several other places, because understanding the business dynamics of organizations and how they run is enormously valuable.

And to have been able to work directly with guys like Steve Ross and Rupert Murdoch and Burt Roberts at MCI was just incredibly valuable.

**_Looking down the road, where do you feel the Internet is going, and where do you feel your business fits within that?_**

I firmly believe that the Internet is quickly becoming the centerpiece of all communications, information, and transactions, thus forming an enormous backbone of our economy. Having come out of the television business, there is no question in my mind that television signals will be transversing the Internet. And we will be using the Internet as the transport mechanism for visual media and oral media—we already do it for the written media.

On the personal communications side, the Internet is unbelievable in terms of keeping up with people in a way that you could never do on the telephone. You can carry on so many more business conversations. You can run your business so much more aggressively and quickly than you could any other way. Being able to set up your company with email and its own intranet—that's enormous.

Certainly, information transactions are already happening on the Net, and we're seeing more and more business transactions happening as well. In short, the Internet is definitely penetrating the economy, and it will ultimately dominate the key forces of communication, information, and transactions.

For us at About.com, that means firmly placing ourselves right in the center of that nexus to be the leader of targeted marketing on the Internet. Because we are able to reach customers, buyers, and sellers alike, we can also bring them together to communicate and, ultimately, consummate a transaction. And that's how we'll take a piece of all of the traffic that moves across the network.

*Computers make it
easier to do a lot of things,
but most of the things they make easier to do
don't need to be done.*

*— Andy Rooney*

# 3

# ask dr. tech

*Answers to some of cyberlife's
most puzzling questions*

PERSONAL COMPUTERS are like cars. In the beginning they
work just fine, but, over time, they give you problems. If that's
true, then ask dr. tech just might be onto something. Here's a
site that offers a service which closely parallels roadside service
for automobiles.

For example, your car breaks down in a cold parking lot on a
Sunday afternoon—"who you gonna call?" Well, for those of us
signed up with AAA or another 24/7 emergency service, help is
just an 800 number away. This is the same concept that ask dr.
tech has applied to the small-time operator.

Most small businessses don't have the techie down the hall or
the help desk that large organizations have. And, while tech
support generally comes with a computer as part of the purchase package, there's often a downside. If you have a palm device or a laptop that they didn't make, forget it. Also, some of
them don't handle specific problems, such as viruses or email
worms.

Clearly, ask dr. tech is another example of entrepreneurs taking
stock of unmet needs in the new economy. Needs such as tech
support are the basis for a new service business—a business that

fills a niche. The service is ideal for the "work anywhere, any-time" freewheeler—the independent consultants or self-employed road warriors who depend on the Web to conduct their business. They can't afford to have any down time due to computer problems. They need someone to call, and they're willing to pay for it. That's where ask dr. tech comes in.

What's attractive about this type of business is the continual source of income from happy customers. As long as the service relationship is valuable to them, customers will renew their subscriptions. The company doesn't have to sell all over again every period like ad-driven revenue sites do.

William Lam started the company in the environs of tech central—Silicon Valley. He first targeted local areas with coffee cup sleeves imprinted with an ask dr. tech logo, and got the service going. He then expanded to other regions in Northern California and got the business growing. Today, anyone can subscribe to the service from anywhere in the United States.

We spoke to William Lam to find out about his new business.

### Can you tell us about your firm and what one finds when he or she visits your site?

My company, ask dr. tech, was founded in April of 1999 to address the significant growing need for technical support. The idea came to mind while I was still the CEO of DSi, Inc., the first company I started. This was in December of 1998. In January, I got together with a Web developer at DSi, along with a friend of mine (another programmer), and began mapping out the tools and infrastructure needed for the company.

The adoption of personal computers in everyday life has revolutionized the way we live, learn, communicate, play, and conduct business. Small businesses and individuals are increasingly dependent on technology to improve their productivity. The advancement of technology has touched the lives of individuals and businesses that never felt the need to adapt, never felt technically competent, or never were able to afford a personal computer before.

The number of personal computer users has grown dramatically, while at the same time technology choices have become more complex. The decreasing prices of computers have forced many manufacturers to limit the level of support provided. This combination has made the availability of technical support more elusive for consumers and small businesses.

Our mission is to be the leader in providing subscription-based technical support services by being faster, friendlier, and more affordable. We provide our support services and other benefits to computer users through a membership program, similar to AAA for automobiles. Once someone enrolls as a member by paying an affordable membership fee he will enjoy the ability to access the help and support he needs 24 hours a day, 7 days a week, so that he'll never be stranded with a computer problem again.

Our service includes online support, which includes self-help tools, email support, and live chat (allows members to communicate with our expert support agents). We also include access to telephone support 24 hours a day for those who want to pick up the phone—maybe because they couldn't get online (i.e., PC won't boot or modem won't work) or they want to hear a friendly voice to guide them through the problems. Our premier members also enjoy the peace of mind of knowing that their equipment is covered by ask dr. tech against theft, loss, or even vandalism caused by viruses or hackers. The equipment is covered for up to $25,000.

**How did the firm and its site come to be? Is there an interesting story behind your start-up?**

Recognized as being computer savvy by all my friends and relatives, I would always get cries for help—at all hours of the day. It was immediately clear to me that the need is out there. It wasn't just because technical support was unavailable, but also because many people had bad experiences with the standard support received with their products, such as long hold times, unfriendly agents, being talked down to, and even finger pointing.

In many cases, a hardware vendor will blame the software and the software vendor will blame the hardware. So I began to put my passion and thoughts into a business idea that will reinvent technical support itself and how it is delivered—faster, friendlier, and more affordably.

**Can you tell us about some of your customers?**

Our customers are people who depend on machines to improve productivity or to stay competitive. They are people who are in need of help from experts who know more than they do when these machines fail or do something they don't understand.

Anyone who uses a computer can benefit from our membership services, but the biggest need is from individuals and small businesses that don't have a formal help-desk department in place. This ranges from soccer moms to independent contractors, small offices, home businesses, and many more. We even have traveling executives and larger companies purchase membership because they need around-the-clock accessibility. Imagine that it's midnight, you're preparing for an 8 A.M. presentation, and your laptop acts up. Who are you going to call?

**Looking back, what were some of your biggest obstacles when just starting out?**

The biggest obstacle in launching a new company, including my own, is generally financing. Now that you have a plan, how much money will you need and where will you get that money? We were fortunate that we were able to do two important things: One, was the ability to begin developing the tools needed to execute our plan, and two, was success in presenting our vision and plans to investors who understood the immediate and long-term need for our service.

**What have been some of the biggest victories you've experienced in taking the site to where it is now?**

One of our early big victories has less to do with our site, but more to do with a phone number. We knew that we had a strong brand with potential, but in order to effectively build on it, we had to not only own the askdrtech.com domain name, but also the phone number. It took us almost three months to successfully negotiate and acquire 1-800-ask-dr.tech, and we were able to do it on a start-up budget.

**If you had to do it all over again, are there things you would do differently to bring the business to where it is today?**

No. I don't regret any choices that I've made. Every single decision may not have always been the best one, but even the occasional bump in the road has allowed myself and my team to learn from it, and ultimately made us even stronger.

No business start-up is easy, yet so many people in this world have a passion for a business of their own. For someone wanting to start an Internet business, what could you offer as advice?

Starting a business is about building—building a concept, building a plan, building a team, and building your customer base. It is all about building, and building something is always hard work. It is important going in that you are ready and dedicated to the commitment and hard work required to build each and every block of your vision.

*If I were a fly on the wall in your offices, what would I find?*
*Do you have a normal office with a dress code?*

You'd find that people can be energized and motivated to do great things. Put a group of energized and motivated people together, and they'll perform the unimaginable.

We don't have a dress code, but I do expect my team to be presentable. I do believe in the term "dress for success." We do have a normal office with a normal water cooler. We have normal people who come together as a team to produce "un-normal" results!

*Can you think of any individuals, books, or even other business ventures that served as inspirational models for your business?*

Yes, I am very fortunate to have great leaders as my mentors. They share with me their experiences and wisdom. I have the advantage of learning about many successes and mistakes even before I'm confronted with them. It is their wisdom that gives me guidance and propels my energy to demonstrate success. Alexander the Great once said, "It is my parents who gave me life, and my teachers who fulfilled it."

*Where do you think the Internet is heading, and how will your site be affected?*

The Internet will always be here. It is an amazing infrastructure that has allowed for real-time exchange of information. It will continue to help people stay closer, work better, and learn faster. Our site allows us to leverage the Internet's ability to share information quickly with both our support agents and our customers.

# 4

# Ask Jeeves Inc.

*Curiosity hasn't killed this cat*

ANYONE WHO BELIEVES THAT icons and images can't create identity in cyberspace needs to visit AskJeeves.com. The site is a search engine with panache—a colorful, well-designed platform for asking any question you'd like. The home page is overshadowed by "Jeeves," the proper Internet butler, who acts as your concierge to the information powerhouse of the World Wide Web.

Pose a question and Jeeves comes back with a list of links that might be able to satisfy your curiosity. The site has used some interesting marketing tactics, including the use of promotional stickers on bananas and apples. In addition, you may have heard its radio ad, which features Jeeves touting the site's capabilities in a proper British voice.

The site has taken the ordinary search function and made it a bit extraordinary. In so doing, it has built a brand image that attracts advertisers and, of course, Web surfers. We spoke to Rob Wrubel, who was instrumental in starting the company, and asked him to tell us more about his company's story.

**Tell us about your firm and what one finds when he or she visits your site.**

Ask Jeeves is a leading provider of intuitive, intelligent Web interaction solutions, delivering a humanized online experience. The company's mission is to simplify people's lives by supplying fast access to answers and to enable companies to maximize the lifetime value of their customers. To date, Ask Jeeves has deployed its award-winning technology and unique expertise in finding answers to billions of questions.

From the beginning, Ask Jeeves—at Ask.com—has allowed users the ease of interacting on the Web the same way they do offline. Users pose questions in plain English and receive links to websites containing relevant information, services, and products. Ask Jeeves' combination of natural-language question answering, human editorial judgment, and popular technology gives users the benefit of millions of previous searches. Growing smarter with each interaction, Ask Jeeves provides targeted, relevant responses to user queries. This simple, straightforward approach has made Ask Jeeves' Web properties—Ask Jeeves at Ask.com, Ask Jeeves for Kids at AJKids.com, and DirectHit.com—some of the most highly visited sites on the Internet.

Deploying the same technology while using the same personal approach that has made Ask Jeeves at Ask.com one of the Web's most popular sites, Ask Jeeves Business Solutions are used by some of the world's leading companies for target marketing, e-commerce, and e-support. With Ask Jeeves' intuitive self-service solutions, companies can convert online shoppers to buyers, reduce support costs, understand customer preferences, and improve customer retention.

### How does your site generate revenue?

Ask Jeeves offers intuitive, intelligent, natural-language, question-answering technologies and services for companies seeking to target, acquire, convert, and ultimately retain customers online. We deliver our services through our Business Solutions and our Web properties. Revenues from our Business Solutions are derived from the licensing of our technology for use on other companies' websites. These revenues consist of three components: professional services, maintenance, and usage fees. Revenues generated from our Web properties (Ask.com, AJKids.com and DirectHit.com) also consist primarily of three components: advertising revenues, e-commerce lead-generation revenues, and dynamic customer targeting and acquisition solution revenues.

### How did the firm and its site come to be? Are there any interesting stories behind your start-up?

David Warthen and Garrett Gruener founded Ask Jeeves in 1996 with a mission to humanize the online experience by improving the way people connect to relevant information, products, and services. The Internet was, and still is, an enormous, confusing mass of information that is difficult to mine for relevant content. Warthen and Gruener recognized an incredible opportunity to create a friendly, approachable service on the Web that would allow people to ask questions in plain English and immediately be directed to relevant answers. And so, Ask Jeeves was born.

Though the founders considered a number of characters to represent the service, they felt that Jeeves the butler was most appropriate. Because the company was dedicated to providing an efficient and relevant service, the founders thought a butler was more fitting than a cowboy, a magician, or a ringmaster. Their instincts were correct. Ask Jeeves has built a lasting and powerful brand around the friendly butler and the notion of personal service he embodies.

Ask Jeeves introduced Ask.com, its consumer question answering service, in 1997. In 1998, Ask Jeeves launched its Business Solutions to deliver question answering services for company websites.

**Can you tell us about some of your customers? Are they individuals or businesses? Where are they from?**

Ask Jeeves created its Business Solutions when industry leaders such as Dell and Compaq wanted to replicate the Ask Jeeves experience on their own sites. Ask Jeeves Business Solutions was launched in late 1998, quickly becoming the technology market leader in online personal service by signing deals with Iomega, Toshiba, and Micron.

Leading companies in the financial services, e-tailing, telecommunications, and automotive industries—including E*Trade, Barclay's, Datek, Nike, Martha Stewart, Airtouch, Nortel, Ford, and DaimlerChrysler—soon followed suit, incorporating the Ask Jeeves experience into their sites. In April 2000, Ask Jeeves launched another suite of services designed for portals, infomediaries, and online marketplaces. The Syndication Services help customers such as Lycos, AT&T WorldNet, MSN, Go2Net, and About.com increase e-commerce and advertising revenue by providing a highly relevant navigation and shopping experience.

**Can you describe some of the bigger obstacles that faced your company in getting off the ground?**

Ask Jeeves' greatest challenge has been managing explosive growth. Evolving from 100 to over 700 employees within one year has required the company to oversee dramatic revenue and systems growth and to create an infrastructure for sales, marketing, account management, and all the other components of a company with global reach.

**What about the victories you've experienced in taking the site to where it is?**

In three years, Ask Jeeves has grown and changed considerably, evolving from a natural-language, question-answering service to an online customer interaction infrastructure company with more than 140 corporate customers composed of numerous Fortune 500 companies. It now features a full technology product line and an immensely popular Web property at Ask.com, receiving more than four million questions a day and holding a top-twenty ranking among Web properties worldwide.

Through grassroots and unconventional marketing campaigns, Ask Jeeves has built a strong brand centered on the character Jeeves the butler and the concept of personal service. Jeeves was the first Internet character to be included as a float in the Macy's Thanksgiving Day Parade, an event that touched 75 million consumers through television and print coverage, helping catapult Jeeves into stardom.

In conjunction with the Fruit Label Commission, Ask Jeeves labeled 275 million apples, oranges, and bananas with stickers featuring Jeeves, the Ask.com URL and an appropriate fruit-related question. Ask Jeeves "butler blasts" have taken place in six major cities across the U.S. and in Sydney, Australia. These guerilla-marketing events feature a group of costumed Jeeves look-alikes who go to high-traffic areas to interact with the public, hand out fun Ask Jeeves items, and inform people about Ask.com.

The 20-person start-up of yesterday has transformed itself into a highly leveraged global business with more than 750 employees in six offices located in Emeryville, Oakland, Los Angeles, Boston, New York, and London. Ask Jeeves International, founded less than one year ago, has successfully formed three joint ventures: Ask Jeeves UK with Carlton Granada, Ask Jeeves Japan with TransCosmos, and Ask Jeeves en EspaZol with Univision. Within its first month following launch, Ask Jeeves UK became a top-ten site in its market.

**Is there anything you would have done differently in bringing the business to where it is today?**

The success we have seen at Ask Jeeves in these few years is related to the brilliant people, products, and programs that form the company. However, our success is not dissimilar to that seen by other companies during the same phenomenal growth period of the "Internet economy."

Within just six months, we have seen a shift to industry consolidation and more conservative growth. Our key for future success will be efficient growth, accomplishing the same great results and expanding the company without overutilizing resources.

*No business start-up is easy, yet so many people in this world have a passion for a business of their own. For someone wanting to start an Internet company, what could you offer as advice?*

Begin with a great idea, something that fills a void or improves upon an existing product or system for consumers and/or companies. Hire talented, creative, and committed people. Then, maintain the enthusiasm and dedication of employees to build the company together and make it successful. Throw yourself into the work, yet set a good example of balance for employees, emphasizing that social, family, and philanthropic activities are important as well.

*What's it like in your offices? What would I find? Do you have a dress code? Water coolers?*

Ask Jeeves has always been proud of the unique culture that has pervaded the company over the last three years, despite changes in size, location, and management.

The richness of company culture at Ask Jeeves is due to a number of factors. Among them is our CEO Rob Wrubel, who is a motivational force for our company; the character of Jeeves and how employees rally around him; and the fact that those working at Ask Jeeves truly believe in the service they are providing.

Listed below are other unique events, practices, and traditions at Ask Jeeves, from beer bashes to Jeeves cutouts. They all contribute to keeping the "Jeeviant" spirit alive.

- I personally use email to break exciting news, address company wide concerns, or give a friendly update on various company activities.

- Office decor is colorful and vibrant, with abundant Jeeves paraphernalia around.

- Thematic parties—from Cinco de Mayo picnics to Valentine's Day barbecues. The Ask Jeeves Communications and Human Resources teams are constantly planning company get-togethers.

- Regular off-site team meetings that strengthen team members' relationships and generate new ideas.

- Great parties! Ask Jeeves throws a wide variety of parties, from low-key company barbecues to flashy events in San Francisco. They are all well-planned, first-rate events designed to raise company morale and project an image of quality to the public.

- Recently, I rented out the Grand Lake Movie Theater during tense times just prior to going public. A company meeting was held followed by a private viewing of *The Phantom Menace*.

- Ask Jeeves employees come from a wide variety of backgrounds, from former Ph.D. candidates to rave DJs, all contributing their unique personalities and perspective to the environment.

- Company dress is casual and reflects the personalities of those who work here.

- Employee community email lists enable employees with similar interests to connect with one another.

- All Ask Jeeves conference rooms are named after famous butlers.

- The best coffee in the area, Peet's, is served with breakfast for all employees every Monday morning.

- Butler Bucks is Human Resources' incentive program to encourage employees to forward qualified candidate's resumes. Employees are financially rewarded if the company hires someone they recommend.

- As an East Bay company, we have retained a lot of Berkeley-style qualities, are involved in local activities, and have happily remained at a distance from the mayhem of Silicon Valley.

- Philanthropic activities include endowing the Ask Jeeves Planetarium at the Chabot Space and Science Center and contributing to the National Center for Family Literacy.

**Are there any leaders, books, or other business ventures that served as inspirational models for your business?**

Scott Kurnit, chief executive of About.com, acts as my shrink, and I often ask him over for dinner. We talk about everything, from employee morale to hiring. I say to Scott: "Oh, are you having a hard time recruiting salespeople? Me, too." Talking with him gives me a sense of which things are actually hard to execute and which are just my own personal challenges.

**Looking ahead, now, where do you see the Internet going? And, in particular, where do you see your site going?**

Ask Jeeves has a tradition of working on the forefront of technology and innovation. As we've watched more of our competitors attempt to copy our success with natural-language technology, we've been striving to carry our paradigm of helping people access information into emerging technologies.

We are currently working to extend our platform into a voice, wireless, multimedia, and multichannel service. By leveraging what we've accomplished in connecting companies such as Dell and Nike to their customers, we're also moving deeper into the B2B space by helping companies manage their supplier, vendor, sales, and employee infrastructures.

Basically, Ask Jeeves wants to provide individuals and companies with the answers they need, at the time and in the form that are most convenient and effective for them. Today that goal is accomplished over the Web with text and graphics, and through live help and voice over IP. Soon though, we will be providing relevant, quality content through streaming video and a network of other devices.

*Pleasure in the job
puts perfection in the work.*

*—Aristotle*

# 5

# Blink.com

* * * * * * * * * * * * * * * * * * * * * * * * * * * * * * * * *

**Could you please mark that page?**

IF YOU'RE A DEDICATED Web surfer, you have bookmarks. And those bookmarks say a lot about you and who you are. They're your "little black book" of the information highway.

What an idea—creating a parking lot in cyberspace that lets you store those bookmarks and then allows others to search and share your little black book. That's what Ari Paparo thought when he decided to start a company that would capitalize on this concept.

But his story isn't just about the concept of a bookmarking site. His story is interesting because it's all about how a high-flying MBA graduate set out to start a company and the journey he experienced in getting there.

**Will you tell us about your firm and what can be found when we visit your site?**

Blink.com allows you to access your bookmarks from any Internet-enabled device. Most Internet users save their bookmarks locally on the browser of a single computer. Unfortunately, this method falls short in many ways, because your locally saved bookmarks cannot be accessed from any device other than the one they're saved on. In addition, bookmarks are vulnerable to computer crashes; they're not secure from prying coworkers or family members; and they generally suffer from a poor interface and limited functionality. Like email, bookmarks are best accessed through a flexible Web-based interface that is device and platform agnostic.

When visitors come to Blink.com, they are asked to register for the service and upload their browser-based bookmarks. This is a simple process that automatically recognizes each user's browser and copies his or her bookmarks into a secure Blink account. The user then has the option to add tools to his or her browser in order to add new sites into Blink while surfing the Web.

Bookmarks are one of the most overlooked aspects of the Web experience, yet they are extremely important to successfully navigating the Web. Surveys show that one third of Internet users have more than 100 bookmarks and that bookmarks are the number-one way in which Web surfers get to e-commerce sites. Yet there is no way for marketers to reach users through their bookmarks.

Since founding Blink, people have come up to me on numerous occasions to complain about bookmarks and their frustrations over them: "I carry a disk around from job to job with my Netscape bookmark file," or "I lost my bookmarks when I changed jobs," or "I have home and work bookmarks, but I can't combine them." It's unbelievable how many people have these issues.

### How did you come to found this business?

I had the idea for Blink in early December, 1998, during my second year of business school at Columbia [University]. I was in the middle of a grueling week of interviews for consulting companies and wasn't particularly enthusiastic about that career path. I had been looking at doing an Internet start-up, but I was nixing all the ideas that came to me because they had already been done, or they were in industries I didn't understand at all, or they plain didn't make any sense. I don't remember the exact circumstances in which I had the idea except that it really just came to me. The line of logic was pretty straightforward: You have email online. You have calendars online. You have file storage online. Let's put bookmarks online!

Once the idea had been germinated, I spent a couple of weeks mulling it over in my head looking for weaknesses and opportunities. Unlike some of my other ideas, this one seemed to have a lot going for it. I expanded the initial idea of personal Web-based bookmarks to include a community of bookmarks and a bookmark-based search engine. I also began to explore interesting distribution opportunities such as co-branding the service and building a B2B business—all of these things have since come to life at Blink.com.

I spent my last semester at Columbia working on the bookmark project while still interviewing for some jobs. By the time graduation came about I had several job offers and made the tough decision to go the entrepreneurial route and start the business. It wasn't just good idea at the time, I had made some progress. The company's name was WhereIgo.com, and I had been networking like mad to find funding and a tech team.

The tech team in particular was quite a challenge. There aren't any good tech people in New York who aren't already gainfully employed. It's particularly hard to get someone of a high caliber who is willing to noodle around with a pre-investment start-up.

So, in the process of working on WhereIgo, I came across a site offering online bookmarks called Bookmarktracker.com. The name alone tipped me off that this was an amateur operation. I emailed the owner and asked him if he wanted to get serious about the business. It turned out he was a nice young guy in his third year at college in Walla Walla, Washington, and he wanted to talk. I flew him to New York and showed him the town. We made a deal that gave me the right to buy his company if I got financing. In one fell swoop, I got a tech guy and a working prototype to show people.

With that in hand, I made a mad rush for financing. Many people were interested, and I got some verbal offers. When push came to shove, however, it took months and months to get anyone willing to put things on paper. By the middle of the summer, I was feeling like perhaps I had made the wrong choice by not taking a job out of school. Then, through a series of odd coincidences, my girlfriend got an email that read, "Start-up focusing on online bookmarks looking for programmers." I called them up that day, put on a tough negotiating posture, and went to their offices to talk.

Within two days we had a deal. I'd be VP of Business Development of the combined company and would coordinate my marketing and business plan. The company, which later became Blink.com, was founded by some technology professionals who had come up with the idea of Web-based bookmarking at the exact same time as I had. So, it was truly a great turn of events.

**Can you tell us about some of your customers? Are they individuals? Businesses? Where are they from and what do they order?**

Blink has both a consumer (B2C) and a business (B2B) product, so our customers vary. When Blink was founded, we were exclusively a consumer Internet business. Our flagship site, Blink.com, allows users to upload their bookmarks and access them from any computer. It's a free service, supported by advertising and direct marketing based around user's bookmarks.

As Blink grew, we began to receive inquiries from companies looking to license our software to offer bookmarking technology to their user bases. Portals, ISPs, and wireless companies all wanted to gain better access to data about their customers and to offer an integrated, personalized service. This will be a growing portion of the business.

**What were some of the bigger obstacles you faced while working to get the company off the ground?**

Blink was launched at a time when Internet mania was still sweeping the U.S. As a result, it was especially hard to attract qualified employees, get the attention of larger Internet partners, and cut through the clutter of billions of dollar of dot-com media spending. Our media budget just couldn't compare with established companies or offline media companies, and building a business in that environment was quite challenging.

**What are some of the biggest successes you've experienced in taking the site to where it is today?**

Blink has been able to grow its user base at a strong pace while minimizing the total expenditures on marketing. This has been a key to surviving the tough times in the Internet space and convincing investors to continue believing in what we're doing. Specifically, we've been able to build cost-effective distribution channels for our product through partnerships with Homestead, ZDNet, and other leading Web companies without necessarily breaking the bank.

**Do you feel you made any mistakes along the way, and, if so, how would you have done things differently?**

Sure. Every business makes mistakes. I think our biggest mistake was not hiring someone senior to manage the product itself. In the early days we had a number of voices impacting product decisions—not always for the better—and we've made a number of blunders in this area. It's not enough to have a strong tech team, you need to have qualified personnel listening to the customers.

*There are lots of people out there who think an Internet business is the ideal way to go. What advice would you have for these folks?*

In my opinion, you should only seriously consider opening a business in a field you thoroughly understand. Of course, that advice would preclude everyone I know from getting into the Internet, so let me be more clear. You meet hundreds of people who have ideas for start-ups, Internet and otherwise. Most of these ideas are left behind, and with good reason. Starting up a company is an enormously risky venture and the best-written business plan can be torpedoed by any number of factors, from poor market conditions to misunderstanding of customer needs.

The best way to minimize these dangers is to know the market extremely well. And the best way to understand the market is to have experience in it. So, if you're planning on starting an e-commerce site for toys, you better have experience in either the toy industry or the e-commerce industry—or at least in retail in some form. One of my business school professors said it best: "Just because you eat out doesn't mean you can open a restaurant."

*Tell us a little about your office environment. Is it business suits or casual?*

Blink is totally casual by policy and personality. Most of us work in a big loft area and, unlike many Internet companies I've visited, people yell across the room and have impromptu meetings in virtually every available area. The tech folks keep bizarre hours—coming in at noon and leaving at 10 P.M.—while the business people are more traditional in dress, demeanor, and so forth.

*Were there, or are there now, any particular individuals, books, or other businesses that have inspired your company?*

Our CEO, David Seigel, is singularly able to motivate us. He is the driving force in the company and is extremely good at analyzing complex situations and picking appropriate courses.

### Lastly, where do you see the Internet going? How will your company be affected?

The Internet is diversifying, becoming accessible on a multitude of devices and platforms. At the same time, the Web page paradigm is diminishing in importance as users pick and choose types of information to access such as MP3s, automated stock tickers, and so on.

Blink is well positioned for these trends as people will become less reliant on their PCs and more diverse in their Web use. Users will need—and will demand—a personal information solution which is secure and travels between platforms. Bookmarks are the simplest and most transparent way for users to get their information where they want it.

*In preparing for battle,*
*I have always found that plans are useless,*
*but planning is indispensable.*

*— Dwight D. Eisenhower*

6

# BookZone.com

*So many books, so little time*

YOU COULD ARGUE THAT it was the sale of books on the Internet that first blazed the trail for e-commerce. But the World Wide Web is not only an ideal place to sell books; it's also a great place to promote them. That's what BookZone has found, as a site that represents publishers and authors in touting their works of prose.

BookZone is an "Internet presence provider" that hosts a Web presence for publishers and authors while providing links to publishers' and authors' home pages. Its presence is its product.

The concept of a presence on the Web, with links and loads of information, is the baseline for this Internet company. To further find out about its business, Mary Westheimer, the chief executive officer of BookZone and one of its founders, spoke about the company and how it came to be.

**Can you tell us about BookZone, and what one finds when visiting your site?**

BookZone is the Web's largest publishing community. More than 3,300 publishers and other publishing professionals have offered their books and services at BookZone, whether on their own site or in our SuperCatalog, which is our main retail area.

BookZone hosts many sites far larger than its own, but currently our site has about 4,500 pages broken up into the following sections:

- The SuperCatalog is our retail area, where publishers and authors sell their books. Both the titles available in the SuperCatalog and the sites that we host show up in the SuperCatalog's more than 100 categories. Sites have included the Net's largest cookbook site, Books-for-Cooks, as well as the largest audiobook catalog, Audio Editions.

  Our SuperCatalog differs from reseller sites, such as Amazon and Barnesandnoble.com, in that publishers are able to offer their books for sale directly—we take no percentage of their sale. This also means visitors link directly to publishers' own sites, which makes the publishers readily available for reporters, booksellers who buy on discount, and others.

  We no longer host Books-for-Cooks, but we do host Chinaberry, which is one of the largest and most highly respected catalogs for books "and other treasures" for families. We also host the U.S. Holocaust Museum Shop site.

- BookZone Pro is our professional area. It features free articles, links, and resources for publishing professionals, including the sites of organizations such as the Publishers Marketing Association (the largest publishing association in the world), Publishers Association of the West, and the Audio Publishers Association.

  Also included in this area is a reviewers' database, a job bank, classifieds, news, an exclusive interactive crossword puzzle, and a services/supplier directory.

- Literary Leaps is the Net's largest searchable collection of book-related links. Anyone can get a free link in five different categories, or they can opt for "featured status" for a low cost. Leaps is one of the largest searchable collections.

- BookFlash is our electronic news announcement service. Anyone who wants to announce news to the publishing press, reviewers, or librarians can do so in a two-pronged approach. First we post their news release online and submit it to the major robot search engines; then we send it to our 5,300 subscribers.

**Everyone who's started a business has stories of his or her journey. How did Book Zone get started? Any interesting tales of how your firm came to be?**

Just two weeks before my soon-to-be business partner approached me in 1994, I was at a luncheon when someone mentioned the Internet, and I literally turned my head. As a busy book packager, I didn't need anything more on my to-do list, my desktop, or my computer. But when I saw what the Net could do, I got what I call "the chill." Those goose bumps are always a sign to me that something is extraordinarily good, and the Net is just that for publishers.

Later, my partner and I sat down with a blank piece of paper and assessed the challenges facing the industry and how the technology could address them, then began planning the site and our services. Of course, a lot has changed since then, but those were heady times!

**What can you tell us about the initial financing of an entrepreneurial start-up? Is this half the battle?**

My then business partner's company financed our start-up. Having enough capital both to sustain a project and to market it properly is imperative. Case in point: Amazon was not the first book reseller online—books.com claims that distinction—but Amazon has been successful (except for making money!) because it had the capital to drown people in advertising and public relations. You don't have to be an Amazon, though. Smart marketers with a good foundation can make it online.

**What was the most difficult part of getting the business up and running as an Internet business?**

I have seen ventures that don't have a solid business model. If you're selling at a loss, you can't make it up in volume. Taking the time and effort to write a business and marketing plan is essential. In that process, you determine when you should start creeping into the black, and if that doesn't show up in your plan, you can see early on that you must adjust.

One would think that the future of the book in this age of instant electronic information would be falling away. However, if one looks at some of the most popular and successful Web start-ups, they are book related.

**Interest in books appears to be flourishing on the Internet. How do you feel about this? Is there a good future for book marketing and promotion on the Net?**

When videos came onto the scene, many people in the movie business thought it spelled their demise. Actually, quite the opposite is true. Videos have made the film industry more visible and profitable than ever. I think the Internet offers the same sort of opportunity for publishers.

Books are an excellent item to sell online because they are a definable product. No matter where you buy a book, it has the same cover, words, and paper (with some small exceptions). That's easier to sell online than, say, clothes, which might not have the right color, shape, or fabric.

Of course, all sorts of items are selling online now, not unlike what happened with the catalog industry. In the 1960s, conventional wisdom was that women wouldn't buy clothes from catalogs. Now it's a $60 billion business!

In addition to the opportunity to sell printed books, the Internet also offers the chance to sell information, whether it's the entire book in electronic format or bits of information. For instance, we host a joint project of the Audio Publishers Association and R.R. Bowker, featuring the entire text of *Words on Cassette*, the audiobook equivalent of *Books in Print*. It allows people to buy a few searches of the catalog, or a subscription to the entire book, which is in many ways more valuable than a printed version, simply because it is searchable and wastes no paper.

Marketing online is an important aspect of the Net. Services like BookFlash that help publishers get out the news about their books without stamps, paper, or other costs are invaluable. And you can talk directly to your audience, letting them know they can buy the books right from you, which, of course, makes you more money.

***If you could turn back time, what would you do differently with respect to how this business was started and evolved to where it is today?***

When we sat down to plan BookZone, we thought we merely had to come up with a way to solve some of the challenges of this industry. I think, however, that we made too huge a leap for some people. I distinctly remember an industry leader telling me, "Sorry, I don't see the value." Now, he's one of our biggest supporters.

The concept of selling books direct seemed wild; now it's widely accepted. In retrospect, we might have taken smaller steps, bringing our clients along with us. The technology has moved so fast, though, that our approach did give us a jump start.

**What street-smart advice would you give to an ambitious entrepreneur who wants to start a business or bring their business onto the Internet?**

Write a business plan. This can't be overemphasized. It's easy to bump along, but to really make progress, planning is the key.

**On a typical day, what would we find behind the scenes at BookZone? Plush corporate offices? How does it compare to other business environments in America?**

Originally, our offices were modest, but we were bursting at the seams with only five employees. We've since moved into larger quarters and expanded to ten employees in-house. There isn't much to see, just some friendly folks working hard at their computers.

Dress is casual—hey, this is Arizona! We're most concerned with helping our customers, so unless we're in a business atmosphere requiring business attire, it's jeans and shorts around here.

**I'm sure I don't have to tell you that the Internet is changing our lives. Obviously, books and the publishing industry are strongly impacted by it. What do you make of the Internet, what it's done, what it's doing, and where it's bringing us?**

The Internet definitely has the capacity to change the world. If you are emailing with folks, or visiting their sites, it makes it much harder to drop bombs on them. As we gain full-time, speedy access and people get over their needless fears about online security, the Net will become an integral part of our lives. There will indeed be a day that we will look back and say, "Gee, do you remember what it was like before we had the Internet?"

**How has the firm handled all the technical aspects of running the website? Would you discourage someone from**

*putting their business on the Web unless they have some technical knowledge?*

You can start with basic knowledge, but you'd better learn quickly. The Net is getting increasingly sophisticated. Yes, anyone can create a page in HTML, but creating a beautiful, fast-loading, well-functioning page is another matter.

*How long have you been in existence, and what was the toughest part about getting started?*

We started BookZone in 1994, just three years after the Internet was opened to public use and one year after the advent of Mosaic, which made the Web the Net's "killer app."

The toughest part about getting started was the need to "make it all up" as we went along. There were no rules, no precedents. We looked at the industry's challenges and the way the technology could effectively address them, and then came up with a direct sales model. As far as I know, no one has been able to do better than we have.

The other challenge was the need to educate our audience. There were times we literally had to explain what the Internet is. Once Amazon came along, it helped shorten the education process for us, because we could explain how we differ.

*What actually sparked the idea to get a business of this type up and running on the Web?*

It was the idea of my then business partner. He wanted to do something for authors and publishers online because he understood that books are a definable item. As I mentioned earlier, no matter where you buy a book, it has the same words, the same cover, the same paper, and so on. That's a much easier sell than, say, clothes, which have to fit, be the right color, and the right weight, or whatever. It didn't hurt, either, that Internet users tend to be better educated and more literate, not to mention better heeled.

### How does the site bring in revenues? How have these revenues grown?

We are what is called an Internet Presence Provider, or IPP. Our publishers and other publishing professionals pay us to host, develop, and promote their sites. We also sell advertising. Revenues have grown exponentially since our early days.

### At what point did you see that your idea was being well received?

We had a rough patch when the Internet began a steep upward curve because people thought they could do it themselves. Suddenly we were competing not just with others who create Web presences for publishing professionals, but also with everyone else from 9 to 90 who thought they could create a site (some of whom certainly could).

Once, I actually saw a sign tacked on a telephone pole in our neighborhood that read, "Will build your website." The only thing missing was, ". . . for food." As the Web and its users have become more sophisticated, it has become clear that not all websites are created equal. Also, our traffic—9 million visitors per year—and our add-on opportunities for promotion have made us the clear leader in this field.

### How do you gauge how much traffic is coming to your site? How has this grown since you first started?

We run reports weekly. Traffic often spikes right after the first of the year, possibly because of so many people receiving computers for the holidays. Our traffic has grown in excess of 1000 percent.

**What about the publishers? Can you give some examples of publishers who used BookZone and achieved significant results from your site?**

Edward Palmer of Youth-Sports.com, has done very, very well with his site. When he came to us, he had a site that was your basic four-color brochure, although it was quite a lovely one. He's developed the site into an amazing place with excellent sales and results since then. Currently, he's grossing about $35,000 annually.

Another good example is Johnny Hamilton of http://www.pipefitter.com. His site was selling $3,000 worth of product each month just one year after launch.

Teaching Strategies at http://www.teachingstrategies.com is a good third example. It is generating 8 percent of its total revenue from the Web, with two-thirds of sales being made by new customers. The site broke even in just eight months, and the company made a considerable investment in the site.

**Lastly, tell us something about using BookFlash to promote books. Has it resulted in any notable success stories that you can share with us?**

Well, one example is Marcia Hoppers of Monte Santo, who mentioned on a mail list I was on that BookFlash was generating 25 percent of her site traffic. But because we don't require all communications to go through us (the posters' email address, URL, and phone number all appear on the release), we don't hear about every remarkable story that occurs. That may be a weakness of our business model, but we're convinced that direct sales is the way of the future.

*Chance favors the prepared mind.*

*— Louis Pasteur*

# 7

# Business Know-How

*Making a business out of small business can be a big business*

JANET ATTARD WAS ONLINE before the Internet was cool. As an author and writer, she's made a business out of helping small and home-based businesses find one thing that they never stop demanding—information. She's a living example of a pursuit that turned into a livelihood. She's also an example of how a Web business is less risky when it's used to enhance and extend an existing business.

The Web allowed her to branch out into new avenues for selling, distributing, and promoting her books and content. It also enabled her to market other books and products to small businesses, as well as allowing others to advertise to a market that she's built. But she's one of the few persons we spoke to who actually started in the late '80s with what was available at that time. Today, Janet is her own boss and helps others to do the same.

After talking awhile, I had to go back and ask the big question: "How do you make money?" She replied that her site sells both her books and others' books, plus it sells some advertising and licenses some content. A little of this, a little of that. But here's the clincher, as she points out ever so smartly: "We do it all with zero debt!"

Naturally, we were eager to learn more about her business.

### Can you describe your company and what can be found when visiting your website?

Business Know-How (businessknowhow.com) is a website that's set up to help small and home-based businesses succeed. Our goal is to make it easier, more profitable, and less stressful to start, run, manage, and grow a business—online or off.

On our site you'll find information, tools, advice, and resources to help our visitors achieve their business goals. Among the things we offer are how-to articles, checklists, and a business-to-business directory that small businesses use to get their business found and to find suppliers and strategic partners.

A writer may need a Web designer, for instance, while the Web designer might need an accountant, or a landscaper, or a source for handmade soaps to sell on his website. We also have a bulletin board where visitors can ask questions about starting and growing their business.

### Tell us a little about yourself and how you came to found this business.

I've been self-employed for many years as a writer. I was writing about small business for a small, direct mail trade magazine, and I was also writing sales and marketing copy and other materials for small businesses. A publishing company I was writing for decided that all its writers had to either send their work over a modem or go into the publisher's office once a week to retype what they had written onto the publisher's computer system. So, I got a modem. This was in late 1985, and computers did not come with built-in modems.

When I got the modem, it came with a brochure for the two online services: CompuServe and GEnie. I tried both and found they were great sources for research information, not only for writing articles, but also for finding out what customers of my marketing clients were really looking for in products.

In looking around the services, I found a work-at-home forum on CompuServe, but nothing like it on GEnie. I knew a lot about business and working at home. I really liked the online experience and figured it would be big some day. (I figured that would be about 5 years! My timing was a bit off!) And I decided that I'd try to get into this new type of media on the ground floor.

So, I submitted a proposal for a home office and small business "roundtable" to the people at GEnie service. They liked my credentials—plus I had been participating in some of the roundtables there—and they offered me a contract.

I launched the my first forum on August 8, 1988, called the Home Office and Small Business Roundtable—HOSB for short. I launched two other roundtables on GEnie—one called WorkPlace and one for taxes. I also launched a business-to-business database there. In addition, I decided to approach other services that were starting up, and I entered an agreement with America Online in 1990 to run a forum there. We stayed on GEnie until GE sold it in 1995 or 1996 (I don't remember which). We are still on America Online and on its Netscape Netbusiness service.

I set up a website in 1996 because I was starting to get people in my AOL forum asking if I had a website. The name "businessknowhow.com" was available as a domain name, so I grabbed it before anyone else thought of it. (Later, I added .net and .org to businessknowhow.com.)

We used the site mostly for our own testing purposes and put just a small number of articles on the site for the public—just enough so we had something to point to when people asked if we had a website. Once we did that, though, ad agencies started contacting me to see about advertising on the site.

### Where, when, and how did you come up with the idea for your business?

The idea for the business started back in 1988, but it has changed somewhat over the years. Originally our thinking was based on an hourly charge model—people were charged by the hour for using online services, and we got paid a percentage of that time from the various online services we were on. So we geared our business at getting people online and keeping them there for as long as possible. We still try to bring as many people as possible to the services we offer online—through our partners and through our own website—but our business model has shifted to look at multiple revenue streams, none of which are based on hourly charges from users.

### What were some of the biggest obstacles facing your company initially?

The biggest obstacle, looking back, was that there were so few people using online services. Also, computers, modems, and the online services themselves were so expensive to use. I was on GEnie for quite a while before it could claim 100,000 subscribers! By comparison, AOL has over 25 million subscribers today.

As I mentioned, computers were expensive then, too—and so were online services. When I first signed up for GEnie as a subscriber, rates were $35 an hour, daytime. There was one other big obstacle. GEnie and CompuServe—and when it started to be known, the Internet—were all text-based systems and very difficult to learn to use. (Web browser technology made the Internet an effective tool for the masses.)

### Tell us about the biggest challenges you've met and overcome while growing your site to where it is today.

Our site is still separate (at this writing) from our AOL forum. But, in our business history, our major challenges have been obtaining contracts with the commercial online services. (We also ran a forum on the Microsoft Network for several years.) Those contracts have helped validate Business Know-How as a primary source of help and information for small and home-based businesses. They were also "victories," in a sense, because those services recognized early on the importance of small business.

Being a subcontractor for the Air Force has also been a tremendous experience for us. One of the neat things about this relationship is that it pushed us to develop skills we might not have developed as quickly otherwise.

Finally, seeing our website, which is not linked into the AOL forum, surpass 1,000 visitors a day without any real advertising on our part—this has been a significant milestone.

**So, if you had to do it all over again, are there things you would have done differently?**

Sure! The path for growing a business is always easier to see in hindsight. If I were starting this today, I'd take more time to research the real market and focus more on our goals. It's easy to get sidetracked and pay attention to the wrong details about running a business. I'd do what I didn't do in 1988—start with a carefully worked-out business plan.

**We know that no business start-up is easy, yet so many people in this world dream of a business of their own. For someone wanting to start an Internet-based business, what could you offer as advice?**

First, be sure you really have a passion for the business. Just wanting to make a lot of money isn't a good enough reason to start a business. It will be a long time before you see big income, if you ever do, and you'll work more hours for yourself than you ever would for anyone else, so you'd better *love* what you do.

Second, know your industry inside and out. Know the people in the industry, too. Have a clear business model and be flexible enough to shift if things aren't working out. And, be sure your projections are based on reality. The bottom line really is the bottom line.

### What about your offices? Are they normal offices with water coolers and so forth?

That's a laugh! I work from a home office and have a staff of people who work for me from their home offices. My "office" used to be a dining room many years ago, and we've never got around to replacing the crystal chandelier. There's often a cat on my desk. Or, if he wants attention, he stands in front of my computer monitor so I can't see it. Dress code is sneakers and comfortable pants in the office, but traditional business clothes when I attend meetings and conferences or have appointments with clients.

### In your opinion, where is the Internet going? And how will your site be affected?

I don't think the Internet is "going" any place different than where it was going before the press and the VCs "discovered" it. It always was and always will be a wonderful means of communication, research, and marketing. I don't think those things will ever change, though perhaps the way those tasks are accomplished will change.

As far as our own site, I think it will continue to evolve and grow by focusing on our customers' needs and making sure we fill those needs better than any other site.

# 8

# CarePackages.com

*Good things come . . . carefully packed*

IT'S WHAT EVERY DOT-COM start-up needs—a former tug-boat engineer from the Merchant Marine Academy. That was one of the ingredients in the start-up of this dot-com, and it just may have launched a business idea that is off at full speed ahead.

Ryan Moran is a great guy, and he's representative of the new set of Webpreneurs. He's a little daring and a little brainy, with lots of vigor and loads of personality. Talk to him, and you'll immediately see that he has what it takes to build a company that focuses on sending out a lot of good stuff.

His business feeds off the thrill we all get when there's a package at the door—for us! Take the concept to the Web and, in Ryan's words, "you hit the gas pedal full throttle." Here's how Ryan described the building of his company:

**Can you tell us about your firm and what can be found at your site?**

CarePackages.com provides consumers with personalized care packages for every event, occasion, or sentiment. Care packages are the ideal solution to help maintain important relationships with friends, families, and coworkers by simply showing them you care. With hundreds of "theme-ready" offerings to choose from, it is easy to quickly create and send the right message. If you are feeling creative, you can build your own custom care packages by selecting from over 500 quality, brand-name items from companies you know and trust. Consumers can also send free digital CareCards and sign up for a free CareCalendar, an email reminder service that ensures you don't miss any important dates!

**Tell us about yourself and how you came to found this business?**

I guess I would consider myself an active, entrepreneurial type. I graduated from the U.S. Merchant Marine Academy as a marine engineer with the idea of working on commercial merchant ships. Unfortunately, the industry was not doing well, so I left to work shoreside.

Next, I got involved with a consulting firm, where I had the opportunity to assist some interesting technology companies with their business development efforts. It was a blast, so I left the consulting firm to work full time at a premier technology research and consulting group, Gartner Group, based in Stamford, Connecticut. While there, the Internet revolution occurred, which ultimately led me to launch CarePackages.com with my partners.

I enjoy new ventures, creating things, and exploring exciting opportunities. The Internet intrigued me, and I had many ideas of how this new platform could be used to provide value to consumers and businesses. I used to get frustrated being with larger companies when I felt resistance to change. The larger you get, the harder it is to move at Internet speed. Starting my own company allowed me a chance to really hit the gas pedal, full throttle!

**How did the firm and its site come to be? Is there an interesting story behind your start-up?**

My partners and I would regularly get together and roundtable business ideas. We are friends and family (one partner is my brother), and we used to spend weekends together pursuing outdoor adventures like spear fishing, fly fishing, camping, mountain biking, snowboarding, etc. We would bring a laptop on our road trips and dedicate hours (and lots of beers) talking, typing, and working on business plans.

CarePackages was a concept that had been around for a long time, in lots of different forms, but not something that was broadly available in the market. The Internet provided some unique advantages to bring this service to the market in a meaningful manner. The more we explored the model, the more it made sense, and next thing you know, we left our full-time jobs, and we were off to the races!

### How did you get the idea for your business?

As I just mentioned, the idea had been around, but it was never broadly available. I believe the challenge of providing an entertaining and convenient ordering environment was one problem that the Web has addressed very nicely.

Most of us have received care packages at some point in our lives. In fact, I used to get a few myself during my years at the academy, but there was always one major problem in my opinion—I didn't receive enough of them!

The reason? It was not easy to put them together, according to Mom and Dad. It involved stops at multiple retail venues, packing supplies, time to write a personal note, and then standing in line at the post office. My partners and I believed we could use the Internet to make sending care packages fun, easy, and affordable. That is what we set out to do.

### Can you tell us about some of your customers? Where are they from and what do they order?

Our customers are both consumers and corporations. There is a common reason people send care packages, which is to maintain important relationships. This applies to consumers sending to friends and families, as well as businesses, which send our care packages to employees and clients to drive business or show appreciation. These are different markets, but the same need is being addressed by the application of a powerful communications vehicle, CarePackages, to convey high-impact, entertaining, but lighthearted acknowledgment.

**What do you recall were the biggest obstacles facing the company at the beginning?**

Setting up fulfillment operations was one of the biggest challenges. I consider myself very process oriented when it comes to business, but I grossly underestimated the number of steps and moving parts involved in creating a cost-effective, timely, and quality controlled fulfillment operation. Setting up supplier networks, electronic order integration, inventory management, merchant accounts, shipping programs, and the like were huge initiatives.

To compound things, only several months into our launch, our fulfillment partner was acquired, so then we had to move our whole operation across the country to another partner's facility. Just when things had started to settle into a groove, the rug was pulled out from under our feet!

Luckily, the new company is a privately held, multibillion-dollar giant in the industry. It helped us make the transition fast and provided us with a highly scalable operation. But those first eight months were a roller coaster ride. Despite our challenges, we never closed the doors during the entire process—we have been going 24/7 since our launch in 1999.

**Can you give me some examples of CarePackage.com's biggest victories to date?**

In terms of the website, adding new shipping capabilities was a big victory. We changed preferred shipping partners from UPS to the U.S. Postal Service about six months into the business and rolled out a total of five new shipping methods, including next-day service.

We also added the option of same-day shipping on orders received by a specified time. Our new fulfillment center was not set up at the time with manifest and electronic delivery confirmation for priority mail service, so it was a big process to get things updated, not to mention the modifications on the site. Shipping affects everything—pricing, customer service, delivery times, tracking—you name it.

It's amazing how challenging shipping can be for an e-tailer. You have no way to determine the exact weight, box dimension, and distance sent for an item before the checkout process. Even if you did, the time to do calculations is not acceptable in the "e-world," so you have to make a lot of concessions and estimates to figure out charges. It took a long time to get it right, and we continue to tweak the model. But it is running smoothly now, and I would consider it a large victory.

***If you were going to do it all over again, are there things you would do differently to bring the business to where it is today?***

Hindsight is 20/20 of course. I am sure there are things I would have done differently, but I try not to think about that now, as it is counterproductive. I hope to learn from my mistakes and try not to make them again!

But if I had a chance to do it again, I would buy tons of Cisco, Yahoo, and Lucent stocks and dump them at their peak. Then, I'd launch CarePackages from the Cayman islands, where I would be running my virtual business from under the palm trees, drinking a pina colada on the beach. Nice dream.

*No business start-up is easy, of course, yet many people yearn for a business of their own. For someone wanting to start an Internet company, what would you offer as advice?*

Follow your dream, and know that the path to success starts with a good road map. By that I mean if it doesn't work on paper, it's not going to work in bricks and mortar or on the Web. By the way, people may call the Web "virtual," but servers, networks, cables, hosting, site design, and the like cost lots of "real" money. Better to learn that your model doesn't work in a Microsoft Excel spreadsheet than from your checking account!

Again, a great road map or business plan is the key to getting off on the right foot. And use your network of friends, family, and colleagues to act as a sounding board of advisors to help you get started. There's lots of great experience all around you if you are willing to accept it. Listen and use their constructive feedback.

But remember that many people are afraid to take the risk of starting their own company (even though they have always wanted to), so they will pick apart your plan and do anything to find a reason it will *not* work. You need to absorb the useful feedback and weed out the negativism that could stop you from following your ambitions.

*What's the atmosphere like at your office? Is it a normal business office? Any dress code?*

We have a casual dress code, many free spirits, and a lot of hard workers. Everyone has a voice. Sometimes that's hard, but overall it makes the company a lot stronger.

*Business ventures are often inspired by great leaders or other start-up stories. Can you point to any exceptional people, books, or business ventures that helped you define your business ideas?*

There are many big businesses today, from IBM to Barnes & Noble, that started as disciplined small businesses, but eventually grew into amazing success stories. I find these companies inspirational. I am always intrigued with IBM and how it has continued to adapt, change, and evolve to the new economy. I believe IBM is a real leader.

**Looking into the future, where do you see the Internet going? How will your site be affected?**

The Internet is a great thing, but at its core, it is simply another communications platform. It will evolve to where almost anything electronic can communicate with anything else electronic. You'll be able to preheat your oven by calling from your cell phone on the way home from work—everything will be wired to the Internet.

For us, we realized early on that the Internet is just one channel for our business and that phone, mail, and direct sales are all necessary sales channels as well. So, we use the Web as a preferred channel, but it is only one facet of our business today. We will leverage the things the Internet does well, but we're not going to rely on it for everything. That's how a lot of companies have become extinct really fast.

*You can't build a reputation
on what you are going to do.*

*— Henry Ford*

# 9

# Collages.net

. . . . . . . . . . . . . . . . . . . . . . . . . . . . . . . . . . . . . . . . . . . . . . . . .

*A picture is worth a thousand words*

FOR OVER A CENTURY, photographs have enhanced our lives. Kevin Casey's business enhances the way photographs enhance our lives. Learn about Kevin and you'll find it's another case of "you never know where an Internet entrepreneur comes from." From flying aircraft for the Air Force, to oncology development, to the dot-com world, Kevin Casey is proof that it's not always what the business is about, but who is behind it.

Kevin offers some great advice: "Talk to people, connect with mentors, listen, listen more, bounce ideas around, but make your decisions like a surgeon. You can't get the job done unless you cut and deliver a result." Sort of what this book is all about! Kevin provides some great insight into his business journey, and his business is a great testimony to his savvy.

Here's what Kevin has to say.

**First, let's talk about your firm and what we can find at its website.**

Our site offers a warm, personal way for people to extend their best wishes on a special occasion, and our event websites are designed for all guests to see and enjoy the photography that captured that special day. While we can post any event captured by a photographer, most of the events that we post are weddings. We provide a guest book on each site so guests can leave a personal note to the wedding couple.

Some photographers will print the guest book entries and include them within a page in the final photo album. Brides really love this and find it a great way to keep the memory alive. Because we have digitized everything to put it on the Web, we have also developed an offline product. For every event, we create a multimedia CD ROM that displays the pictures from the website. Brides really like this permanent keepsake, and we package it for them in an elegant jewel case.

### Tell us a bit about yourself and how you came to found this business.

During my college summers, I started a housepainting business, which evolved from a one-man operation into a crew of 10 before I had to leave for flight training after graduation. I made more money during those three summer months than I did the whole next year as a second lieutenant! This housepainting experience developed me quite a bit, and it also convinced me that I had the skills and desire to run my own company in the future.

After graduating from Holy Cross in 1984, I flew B-52s in the USAF—to repay my ROTC scholarship—until December 1990. While stationed at Griffiss Air Force Base in Rome, New York, I earned my MBA in management from Rensselaer. I enjoyed the MBA program, especially the case studies. It was then that I decided my desire, skills, and talents would be best utilized in the business sector.

The Air Force life was great, but it was time to move on. I still get a kick out of the guys who actually thought I was nuts for leaving such a comfortable lifestyle. I can't imagine what they'd think when I tell you that Rome, New York, was a great place for my wife Debbie and I to start our family. Today we have a 14-year-old son and a 13-year-old daughter.

After the Air Force, I spent nine years building markets for new diagnostic tests for the oncology market. We introduced PSA testing which is now the standard test for screening men over 40 for prostate cancer. From 1995 through 1999, I also had the opportunity to help revolutionize the PAP-smear market by introducing a new technology that has improved the traditional PAP smear test.

### How does all this experience pertain to starting a website business?

Actually, I think there is a big correlation. These work experiences helped me to develop the marketing and sales skills which I think are so critical to my success today. Marketing and selling stuff isn't difficult. Building successful, high-growth companies stems from good ideas executed by people who know how to raise the awareness for a new concept, idea, or service. It's a process. Sometimes this process can be difficult, but it is also very rewarding.

### How did the firm and its site come to be? Is there an interesting story behind your start-up?

I was in charge of marketing and sales at my previous employer, a medical company, when the husband of a friend of mine in customer service emailed me a picture of their newborn. I was in awe of the fact that this baby was newly born, and here I was looking at the picture just three hours later.

I immediately thought of the possible opportunities associated with building websites for babies and their parents. While I know this is now being done today by some companies, I dismissed it then because I felt the market wasn't really that big. How many pictures of a baby in a hospital crib can you sell?

Two weeks later, though, it dawned on me that the Internet would be a great tool for connecting people who attend special events with the photographs taken during the event that they might never get to see. Wedding pictures, for example. The photographer invests a whole day, the couple spends a lot of money, but no one ever gets to see the pictures. That night I began sketching the initial site on paper. This was February 1999, and I continued planning until I left my job on my wife's birthday, March 26th. Nice birthday present, eh?

I then raised some seed money to keep the process going, developed a website, and talked to photographers. (It's amazing how little you need to live on when you have no income and you don't have to pay taxes.)

My family was a big key to getting my start-up airborne. My kids helped pick the name of the company, and my wife never complained when I took over the dining room, spare bedroom, living room, and, eventually, the kitchen. Luckily, funding became available, and I moved the business out of the house.

It was important to me to involve the kids. They always wanted to help with building boxes and putting kits and folders together. I think they learned a lot from this experience, watching a new company literally unfold in our home. When they get their own great ideas as adults, I think they will be able to see beyond the obstacles because they have a reference point from which to relate.

### Can you tell us about some of your customers? Are they mostly individuals or businesses?

Our customers are photographers, and they purchase from us a website along with an interactive CD-ROM, which they resell to their clients. In short, the company works with professional photography studios to create interactive, personal, e-commerce websites for their clients' special event photos. These event websites are password protected and will display an event's photos for 60 days. During that time, anyone who has the site password can view, email, or purchase the photos of their choice. Currently, there are multiple revenue sources for both Collages.net and the photographer, including personalized client website sales, photo sales, and CD slide show sales. We also partner with professional photo finishing labs.

**What were some of the biggest challenges you faced as you worked to make your ideas reality?**

Pitching our story in the spring of 2000 was difficult, because it was a time when dot-com carnage was just beginning to appear. The March 2000 stock market got people worried, and investors had a real attitude shift in terms of what they were willing to invest in. This was tough.

We were running out of money, I was used to a six-figure income, and I never expected the fundraising would be as time-consuming as it turned out to be. It's very difficult when you have no money left, and you find yourself buying plane tickets to Atlanta on credit in order to visit potential investors. Thankfully, my wife didn't ask too many questions. It could've gotten ugly.

**What about your successes? What are some of the big victories you've pulled off while taking the site to where it is today?**

My brother-in-law, Norm Racine, was "manna from heaven." During the summer of 1999, my sister-in-law showed him the website that I was building. She was an English major in college, so I was having her edit it. When Norm saw the site, he called me up, expressed his interest, and basically dropped what he was doing to be part of the start-up. Since the plan didn't call for capital until the first half of 2000, there was no money to pay him. But Norm was in a position to come on board, make a big sacrifice, and help me get the company moving forward. While Norm earned a good deal of equity during that first year, he also made a great sacrifice in terms of time spent with his three kids. Norm's wife and kids also played a big role in helping us, when they could, with all the details that came up as we strove to complete our mounting pile of tasks.

Norm was so instrumental in helping to complete the many projects that we needed to get done very quickly. We needed to "build our story," test product, and build the business plan. These can be very trying tasks, especially when things don't work out as planned. Norm had a great deal of start-up experience, along with great patience and problem-solving skills. Needless to say, we both tested our skills and abilities in this area.

I didn't plan on Norm joining me, but as I look back, I don't know where we'd be today had he not joined. I count his help and support as a major victory.

Also, Steve Lundy, a good friend of mine from the diagnostics industry, joined just three months ago as our VP of marketing and sales. Steve too has been a great addition to Collages.net. He helped us get the sales force going, contributed with strategic partnerships, and has added great insight to our business in a very short time. Unbelievably, Steve turned down an opportunity to run a $400 million business unit for Johnson & Johnson to be part of our team.

**What would you do differently if you could start the whole process over?**

Raise money more quickly, before the market got too tight. Money was a real problem at first.

**If I wanted to start an Internet business today, what advice would you offer me?**

Well, it's not for everyone, but you might have a good shot if you can do the following:

- Be optimistic
- Be patient
- Be persistent
- Be creative
- Be cautious
- Be persuasive

More specifically, find a partner within your first six months. A great one. One who is willing to commit to the success of the business and also willing to make sacrifices. Next, when you develop your product, don't attempt to radically change the behavior of your customer. Fit your product around what they are comfortable doing today.

Try to learn from your mistakes, and be prepared to change course quickly and unexpectedly. And it's very important to make sure your spouse is on board. Be sure to involve your family, because they too are making big sacrifices.

**Do you have a typical office situation? How are things set up where you work?**

Casual dress is the rule, and we share space with another dot-com to save money. It works out pretty well, though. These guys write jokes for a living, so we have some unique ways to occasionally take down time.

**Can you share your source, or sources, of inspiration for deciding to have your own business? Any special people, books, or business models?**

I think my parents have been my biggest inspiration. They always told me that I could do whatever I wanted to do in life. When you hear this enough, I guess you eventually believe it.

During a sixth-grade parent-teacher conference, the teacher told my mother that I was a born leader, but that I was leading the class in the wrong direction. That, I think, was my turning point. My parents took that opportunity to get me back on course, and I did get serious in high school.

My parents have both been successful because they too believed that they could do whatever they wanted. They balanced work, family, and play, and served as great role models for me in many ways.

My biggest business mentor is Jack Davis, a former Abbott diagnostic VP. Jack built that company, the first that I joined out of the military, from nothing to $100 million. Jack has taught me much about business and was instrumental in helping me secure funding by leading me to another mentor, Bill Longley. Bill sold his company to Healtheon WebMD in late 1999. He has certainly been an inspiration, a source of levity when the going got tough, a great coach, and a "rainmaker" when it came to raising funds.

Also, I like Jeff Bezos because he thinks big—really big. And I've always liked the phrase: "Fortune sides with those who dare."

### Where do you think the Internet is going? And in light of this, where do you see your site going?

The Internet has revolutionized our life and will continue to impact it in ways that we haven't even dreamed of. Until then, those sites that provide a tool to solve a problem, join buyers and sellers in unique ways, and make life easier than the way it was done yesterday—those sites will survive and provide a good rate of return for investors.

# 10

# Culturefinder.org

· · · · · · · · · · · · · · · · · · · · · · · · · · · · · · · · · · · · · · ·

*Classical music, dance, opera, theater, Broadway art
and "all that jazz"*

TAKE A FORMER CELLIST and executive director of the American Symphony Orchestra at Lincoln Center, give him several years of corporate marketing experience at American Express, and what do you get?

Meet Eugene Carr, the president of Culturefinder. Eugene founded and now runs this Internet-based company, which touts itself as "the only online national calendar that includes season schedules for over 4,000 arts seasons and events in the U.S. and Canada, including classical music, dance, opera, theater, Broadway shows, and museums."

Eugene Carr is a true-blue "Webpreneur," who conceived, created, and found success on the Internet. Indeed, his site appears to be humming a fast-paced waltz from a happy musical. We spoke to him to learn firsthand what his stage is all about.

### So, just what is Culturefinder.org?

Culturefinder is the leading service for arts events listings and ticketing on both the Internet at large and America Online. Culturefinder provides the only online national calendar, which includes season schedules for over 4,000 arts seasons and events in the U.S. and Canada. You can search our site by date, by city, or by organization name, and you'll get the full schedule as well as detailed information about each of the events. In addition, you are able to buy tickets directly from us online. So, we're a combination of a ticketing service and a massive event calendar for the arts.

### It's an interesting concept. How did the idea ever come about?

I was the executive director of the American Symphony Orchestra from 1991 until 1996, and as such produced concerts at Carnegie Hall and Lincoln Center on a regular basis, marketing events to an arts-loving public here in New York City. I learned a great deal about what prompted people to buy tickets to events or not to buy tickets, and it was apparent to me that the thing that people wanted more than anything was to know more about each event. Clearly, an advertisement in the newspaper, a few seconds on the radio, or a flashy poster wasn't enough to get by people's fear of the unknown.

In 1994, it became clear to me that the Internet was a place where I could aggregate a massive amount of information that would be of interest to arts patrons whether at home or while traveling, all presented in an easy-to-search format. They'd have the ability to access a great deal of information about the events, which would motivate them to buy tickets.

The idea came to me as I became increasingly aware of what I thought was going to happen on the Internet in 1994 and 1995. I knew that somebody was going to create the arts section of the Internet, but because I already had the idea, I didn't want to wait around for somebody else to beat me to it.

As an entrepreneur over the years, I had already watched several of my ideas come to fruition under someone else's name. I am quite convinced that there are no truly unique ideas—just ideas attached to people who can get them done. So, I just decided to embark upon this project and race ahead before anyone else could get there before me.

### How does Culturefinder generate its revenue?

Our company is based on an e-commerce model. We sell tickets, charge the customers a service fee, and bring in revenue from those service fees. In addition, we have the ability to sell products that relate to the arts, such as posters, CDs, and books. We will eventually sell travel products as well, such as travel packages, a Culturefinder weekend, and that kind of thing.

We also sell advertising on the site. Baldwin Piano was one of our first long-term sponsors, and we have sold advertising to American Express, Lexus, and others. Basically, the concept here is to aggregate an interested audience, which happens to be very upscale, and sell things to them. We provide information that draws these people to the site and, at the same time, offer them products and services that they are interested in. Advertisers willingly pay to have access to that audience.

*I recall the famed value investor Warren Buffet remarking on how even a small community newspaper is in demand because of its "bulletin board" qualities. It provides a place for people to find out what's happening. Would you agree with this? Do you find that there is a sustained demand from people to find out what's happening in their community with regard to cultural happenings?*

I increasingly believe that all information is indeed local when it comes to arts information, which is why we designed our site to offer essentially local information on a national basis. I think people want to know what's happening not only in their own communities, but when they are traveling, too. They want that information easily packaged and accessible. They don't want to work very hard to find it, and when they get there, they want information that's going to be relevant to them in making a decision. I recall looking at our local newspapers when I was growing up and seeing listings for the New York Philharmonic that read: "New York Philharmonic at 8 P.M., Beethoven, Brahms, Schubert." Well, even as a young music student, I knew that wasn't enough information for me to buy a ticket. Why did they list it that way?

**Was there a particular time or place that the vision and concept of Culturefinder as a site on the World Wide Web hit you?**

Yes. I was on a road trip, sort of a soul-searching road trip in 1995. I drove down to visit my college roommate, who's a professor at Duke University. It was while driving to North Carolina that the concept really hit me as one that was viable.

I was searching for some new business ideas, and this seemed, as I said before, obvious. It was an obvious idea, and somebody was going to do it. It didn't occur to me that it was either clever or something that could be protected. I figured there were probably a dozen people out there who had the idea and that I had better get going on it right away. It turns out, though, that I was at least a year or more early, but I did get the chance to get in first.

**Did you have a clear vision of what you wanted the site to look like at the outset?**

I suppose the answer is yes. If you go to our site today and compare it to the original site, they are almost identical in a fundamental way, in that the calendar was always the first and most important element. If you look at our site today, there's a place to search for events, and that's exactly what the site looked like at the beginning.

There was a greater emphasis when we started on straight editorial, which has now taken a back seat to the more utilitarian calendar functions. I think I had pretty good ideas of what functions and information I wanted to post, but I didn't have a graphic idea about it. Then again, there weren't such things as graphics on the Internet in 1995. You were lucky if you had straight HTML and a few cartoon graphics. That was considered site design.

*In your "Backstage" section, you offer a brief profile of yourself which brings to light an interesting background, one characterized by a mixture of art, business, and community service. You've certainly done a variety of things in your life—cellist, board member of a symphony orchestra, developer of a culture program for high school students, and an MBA from Columbia! What drove you to the business side of the arts?*

I found it easier than playing the cello. When I was in my early twenties, I had been practicing and performing for 12 or 13 years. Though incredibly rewarding, it was very, very hard work. I had also dabbled in arts management through my involvement in a youth orchestra and by managing and booking a trio that I had founded at Oberlin College. We performed 125 concerts in 25 cities during our vacations. The business side of it came very easily to me.

As I was mulling over which way my career should go, business seemed the more comfortable thing to do, something I could do naturally, and I decided to make music my avocation as opposed to my central focus. It just seemed that the arts were an area where there was an opportunity to do interesting and creative things, work with interesting people, and, on the business side, to really have a very big say in making something important happen. That was meaningful to me. I never wanted to do something that somebody else had done. I always wanted to do something that was unique, different, and never done before. That's exactly what I've found working at all the arts institutions that I have worked at, and that was certainly the case at the American Symphony.

*Often, a good idea is driven by inspiration. What has in-spired you over the years? Was anyone particularly instrumental in getting you to the position you're in today?*

Well, many people have been instrumental in getting me to the position I'm in today. I'd say I was influenced by people like Joseph Papp, who is responsible for founding the New York Shakespeare Festival. He started with a simple idea of doing Shakespeare in the parks. He brought it to the mayor and ulti-mately founded a major New York production and arts organization, which now lives on with his name and comprises a major force in New York City. That kind of entrepreneurship in the arts seemed attractive to me. I never met him, but it was just what he stood for that was an inspiration to me.

Another person who influenced me greatly is Arthur Zankel. He's a board member of Carnegie Hall, a director of Citigroup, and a founder and partner at First Manhattan. When I met Mr. Zankel through his son Ken at business school in 1987, he en-couraged me to come to him with entrepreneurial ideas. When I brought him Culturefinder in 1995, he became my first inves-tor.

Arthur taught me a big lesson about investors because he kept saying that he was "betting on the jockey, not on the horse." He basically believed that I would figure out how to create an inter-esting business on the Internet. He knew that the business plan that I had presented to him wasn't anything like what we were going to end up with. So, he probably deserves much of the credit for getting me to the position I'm in now.

*Most ventures face a variety of stumbling blocks as they move toward their goals. Can you tell us about some of the real-life obstacles you encountered while taking Culturefinder from its original conception to the grand unveiling of its website?*

First and foremost is money. You know everything takes much more money than you think it will, and even though everyone said to make sure that I had enough money, the reality was that I was never going to have enough money. If I had waited around until I felt I had the appropriate amount, I never would have done anything at all.

Rather, it was the experience I had in the not-for-profit world, which essentially forces you to spend money ahead of raising it, that trained me and gave me the sort of backbone to be able to plow ahead in this business without proper resources. Nonetheless, 20/20 hindsight says that if I had much more money at the beginning, things would have turned out a lot differently.

Beyond this, you have to realize that the Internet has changed fundamentally since we started, and it's been a little bit like building a house on quicksand. The moment you think you've got something that works, the industry shifts and suddenly it's no longer relevant. It's been exhilarating, but complex, to keep up with the changing forces of consumer trends and corporate superpowers that are changing the media.

*I suppose a website such as yours couldn't be produced without the help of others. You now have a staff that works with you behind the scenes in many different areas. How important has this team been in bringing the business to fruition?*

I can't make the claim that I make the site happen. There have been countless people who have helped. People who've worked full-time, part-time, and on a volunteer basis. I don't even know the cumulative number of people who have worked on this site over the years, but I'm sure it's well over 300 people. I'm a collaborative personality, and I like to work with people. I'm not much of a dictator. In fact, I often do my best work with others. If you look at our staff list, you'll see that most everyone comes with some kind of arts background and arts interest. So, we have a very rich, fruitful, and open kind of business environment, where everyone participates and helps create what you see on the screen.

**Where did you find people to work for you and with you on this site?**

New York City is full of arts-interested people, who find working at Culturefinder a satisfying combination of their passion for the arts and what they want to do during the day. I'm fortunate to have ex-dancers, Broadway singers, musicians, conductors, and those kinds of people working for us. It makes for a wonderful office environment.

**What's the best advice you can give to anyone considering an Internet business, or to any entrepreneur for that matter?**

I think the best advice I could give is this: If you feel you have the passion, the drive, and the energy to start a business, then jump into it without overthinking it. It's like any kind of a race. What it looks like at the starting line and what it looks like when you're in the midst of the race are two very different things. You can't predict what the race will look like down the road. All you have to do is decide whether you want to get in it or not.

So my recommendation is to first make the decision. If it's in your blood, go ahead and actually do it. I suppose it's a little bit like having children. Not having children myself, I speak with no experience, however I imagine that the decision to have children is a key decision. Once you've made that decision, you can't necessarily predict what's going to happen. So, if you have the drive and the passion to start a business, make your plans, place your bets, and go do it.

# 11

# Developer's Network

. . . . . . . . . . . . . . . . . . . . . . . . . . . . . . . . . . . . .

## A Web business for Web businesses

BRIAN SHEPPARD IS A TECHIE who has hung out his shingle as an entrepreneur. I must add a caveat, however. By calling Brian a techie, I don't mean to put him or anyone else down. It's what Web-savvy professionals, who know more than most of us, are affectionately called nowadays. It is a compliment, and Brian's "technogeekitry" has enabled him to build a site that everyone reading this book ought to visit. It's a Web-building resource for Web developers.

It all started on a beach in Jamaica. After leaving his full-time job, Brian describes the beginning of his next career: "I spent two weeks in Jamaica, and then came back and devoted myself full time to the Web development business." He later adds, "After that, it was sort of evolutionary." Well, isn't that the story of life? Listen to Brian's story as he describes how his business came together.

**Tell us about your firm and what we can find when we visit your site.**

DevelopersNetwork.com is a site for Web developers and other Internet professionals. We provide information, tools, resources, and answers for people who are developing any kind of website, including e-commerce sites.

When people visit our site, they find four major items. They find listings of the top companies in various arenas, such as hosting companies, e-commerce firms, dedicated server companies, and the like, plus a domain name search and registration tool. They also find articles on development issues, including new technologies and popular website features, which help both new and experienced developers stay up-to-date in this rapidly changing industry. They also find our expert Q & A feature, Ask Einstein, where they can ask specific questions and get an email response.

### Can you tell us a bit about yourself and how you came to found this business?

I guess you could say I'm a veteran entrepreneur, if there is such a thing. This is the third Internet start-up I've founded, although it sort of evolved from the first two. I studied computer science and economics at the university, so I guess starting a technology business was sort of inevitable.

### How did the firm and its site come to be? Is there an interesting story behind your start-up?

I started my first Internet business (developing websites) on a part-time basis while I continued to hold a full-time job. That was the situation for about six months, but the company I was working for had begun to make some changes. So, I decided to leave my full-time job and take two weeks off to go to Jamaica. When I came back, I concentrated exclusively on my Web development business.

Many of my Web development clients were looking for Web hosting services, so I started a Web hosting company as well. Because there were fewer Web hosting companies than Web development companies at that time, the hosting side of the business grew, and I began to focus on that. As that business grew, I needed more money to spend on advertising to attract new clients, so I started a site call Developer's Directory, where employees in charge of finding a Web development firm could search our database of such companies. At the same time, we promoted our Web hosting services to the development firms in our database. Developer's Directory was so successful, I decided to expand it, and it ultimately became Developer's Network.

**Where, when, and how did you get the idea for this business of yours?**

I guess the genesis would have to be on that beach in Jamaica, after I left my "day" job and decided to go into Web development full time. After that, it was sort of evolutionary.

I think the interesting story is that the company and site that are now Developer's Network evolved from a part-time Web developer who took advantage of a series of opportunities in the marketplace. When my clients needed hosting, I chose to provide it rather than send them somewhere else (partly because I didn't know where else to send them). Then I realized that other developers were probably in the same boat—not knowing where to go to find resources for their clients—so, the need for a site like Developer's Network became obvious.

**Tell us about some of your customers. Where are they from and what do they order?**

Our customers fall into three major categories: Web developers, small business owners, and Web-hosting companies (particularly dedicated hosting companies). The Web developers and small business owners use the site as a resource to find companies that offer the products and services they need to complete their Internet strategies. They also buy domain names from us. The Web-hosting companies are our advertising clients.

**Looking back, what were some of the biggest obstacles facing the company in getting off the ground?**

Not surprisingly, the biggest obstacles we faced were business related, not technical. Most people who start up a business pay the most attention to the product or service they are offering, but the area that can cause the most trouble is the business of business. In other words, I started this business because I understood the technology. Where I needed help was with the business side of it.

That said, the three areas that proved to be the biggest obstacles were staffing, time management, and money. As far as staffing went, I could find people who were technically good, but finding people who shared my dedication was more difficult. That's understandable, of course, because it wasn't their company.

Time management continues to be an area in which I struggle. Like most entrepreneurs, I tried to do it all at the beginning, so I never had time to do things right. Delegation is a very difficult, but very necessary, thing to learn. And money is likely on everyone's list of obstacles—there's never enough to grow as fast as you want, and finding it takes up more time than you expect.

**Tell us about your biggest victories as you've taken your site to where it is today.**

Just the fact that the site *is* where it is may be the biggest victory for me. Being seen as a comprehensive resource for developers, Webmasters, and small businesses is really what we set out to do, and I think it's safe to say that we've accomplished that. The fact that we continue to grow—in hits, in advertising revenues, and in recognition from the development community—is also a big victory.

**Are there things you would do differently if you could start all over again?**

I think I'd try to start with some money! Because I didn't intend to create Developer's Network, I pieced together the financing as I pieced together the company. If there's a next time for me, I'd like to begin with a brilliant idea and solid financing. I'd also hire a proper management team from the beginning—people with track records in the industry. Of course, having the financial backing would make that task a lot easier too. I would also use a personal and business coach to help me deal with the myriad issues that arise with any start-up business.

**No business start-up is easy, yet lots of people still want a business of their own. For someone wanting to start an Internet company, what can you offer for advice?**

As I mentioned, money and good management are key. If you can assemble a crack executive team and secure financing, you're halfway there. Of course, there are many companies that succeed without those two key factors, effectively pulling themselves up by their bootstraps. In those cases, and in well-funded and well-managed start-ups as well, perseverance is key. Believe that you can do it, then go out and do it.

I would also advise anyone who has grown a business to the point where they've moved out of the garage to seek the counsel of a personal and business coach for any issues they're unprepared to deal with. There will be many!

**Tell us a little about your office environment. Do you have a dress code, water cooler, and so forth?**

We do have a water cooler, but there's no dress code to speak of. We order food from Grocery Gateway every week, which the company pays for. We also have the obligatory foosball table and flexible work hours. I guess the corporate culture, if you will, is pretty developer-centric, because many of our employees and most of our customers are developers.

**Many business ventures are inspired by great leaders or other business start-up stories. What inspirational books,**

*leaders, or other business ventures did you look to when putting together your business?*

I found Steven Covey's *Seven Habits of Highly Effective People* to be very inspiring, as well as Anthony Robbins and his books on personal achievement.

**What do you think the future of the Internet is going to be? And how will your site be affected?**

I believe that we are only at the beginning of the Internet shake-out and that those companies with weak business models will disappear over the next three to twelve months. Users will become more educated and more discriminating about the sites they utilize.

In order to meet these challenges of the maturing Internet economy, Developer's Network will remain focused on our long-term business model. That means continuing to focus on providing the most comprehensive resources for Internet professionals, as well as maintaining the flexibility to add new services as the need arises. After all, that's what started the whole thing!

# 12

# eHealthInsurance.com

. . . . . . . . . . . . . . . . . . . . . . . . . . . . . . . . . . . . . . . .

*There are currently 44 million persons in the U.S. who lack health insurance*

VIP PATEL AND HIS TEAM have built an online solution called eHealthInsurance.com that is working to reduce the number of uninsured through its nationwide offerings. By visiting this site, you'll be able to find all the information crucial to making the right health insurance purchasing decision for yourself and your family. Ultimately, you'll be able to say what so many can't: "I'm covered."

As Patel states: "Our purpose is to help people who need health insurance by reducing the complexity and uncertainty of the health insurance purchasing process so they can get the plan that is right for them, their family, and/or their employees."

Listen to Vip Patel as he tells it like it was, and is, in building his business:

**Can you tell us about your firm and what can be found on your website?**

On our website (www.ehealthinsurance.com), individuals, families, and small businesses alike have the opportunity to learn about, compare, apply for, and buy health insurance online from the nation's leading health insurance carriers. Our company's number-one priority has always been customer care, so in addition to all of the information provided to consumers on the website, eHealthInsurance also offers the assistance of licensed, unbiased health insurance specialists who are available via live online chat, email, or phone.

At www.eHealthInsurance.com, a visitor will have the choice of getting individual or family insurance, small business insurance, or medical supplemental insurance for seniors. Visitors only need to enter a few pieces of information before they are able to use our customer-friendly tools, such as online instant quotes, side-by-side comparisons of plan prices and benefits, and online physician directories. These tools provide useful, unbiased information to help visitors select the health insurance plan that best meets their needs.

Additionally, we are working with our insurance carrier partners to reduce the amount of paperwork associated with getting health insurance by using new technologies, such as digital signatures and online payments to speed up and simplify the process for our customers. In this way, eHealthInsurance is able to deliver faster health plan approvals.

**Let's talk about you for a minute and how you came to found this business.**

After graduating from Stanford, I was unemployed, and while looking for a job, I bummed a place to stay—on the floor of a friend's place! I was eating mostly canned foods, and I somehow contracted food poisoning that went on for weeks. When things finally got bloody and extremely painful, I swallowed my pride and went back to the Stanford student health center. They said they couldn't help me and then directed me to the county hospital because I was *uninsured.* Instead, I went back to the floor of my friend's place and waited for things to get worse before they got better.

Years later, my uncle, who came from India to run a business here, had a stroke. He had no health insurance, didn't know where to get it, and was only able to get the care he needed by returning home. These and other personal incidents sparked a passion in me for improving our health care system in the U.S., especially for the uninsured.

This passion and my career path began to converge several years later. I graduated from business school and joined a then no-name company called Silicon Graphics (SGI), founded by Jim Clark, a former Stanford professor. After my five years at SGI, Jim had left to found Netscape, and I decided to look for a change myself. During business school I interviewed, unsuccessfully, with only one venture capital firm. That was Kleiner-Perkins, known as "the king of VCs." My idea for the next step beyond SGI was to join a Kleiner-Perkins-funded company with the thought that I might learn the right way to build a start-up.

So, at a public event I sought out John Doerr, cofounder and president of KP, and asked how I might join a KP-funded company. In a pleasantly warm manner, he asked in return about what I wanted to do and what was in my heart? In my heart was the genuine thought that it would be meaningful for me to somehow use technology for societal benefit, specifically in health care. Surprise of all surprises, he pointed me to Jim Clark, who was about to launch another venture backed by Kleiner-Perkins, called Healthscape (later named Healtheon/WebMD). That same day I spoke with Jim, and he gave me the name of a contact person there.

When they didn't return my call, I spoke to Jim again, and this time he placed a personal call on my behalf to the president. Even though the only health care experience in my background was that I was in the "cohort" focused on health care at Wharton, the door was opened for me to become a very early employee at the new start-up. Somehow, in one step, I had landed an opportunity to possibly make some serious money, to learn how to build a start-up, and, most importantly, to follow an interest and a passion that was in my heart.

### How then did your firm and its site come to be?

My wife, Sharon, was the seed capitalist when she agreed that I could go cold turkey for six months without an income to attempt the start-up. Sharon was also responsible for recruiting our first engineer, Carmine Rimi, from KIVA/Netscape, and he managed to build eHealthInsurance.com with only a small team.

When the company's revenue started flowing in, Sharon left her job in charge of national sales training at Octel/Lucent to join the start-up, wearing a broad range of hats from network administrator to marketing communications coordinator to product marketing manager, even finance director and HR manager. She became so valuable that only her pregnancy was sufficient justification to let her leave the pressure cooker. Of course, employees continued to call her at home for assistance.

The start-up phase depended much on the help of family, friends, and friends of friends. In addition to Sharon, a brother, a cousin, an uncle, and other family members provided key assistance. Donations of the first furniture, office space, cabling the office, database schema design, press kit preparation, user-interface consulting, logo design, recruiting, product marketing ideas, VC preparation, and more came from people who wanted to help with little or no expectation for anything in return. Without these people, there's no way the company could have taken off.

### Tell us how and when you got the idea for your Internet business.

The business opportunity for eHealthInsurance is the online sale of the largest product segment—health insurance—within the nation's largest industry—health care. This discovery did not come in a vacuum.

The premise of Healtheon came from John Doerr and Jim Clark, who jointly decided that it made immense sense to find ways to use the most revolutionary technology in decades, the Internet, to address needs in the nation's largest industry, health care. They applied a standard start-up formula that consisted of applying money and smart people to a business problem and then telling them to go figure it out.

As the one charged to go figure out future Internet-related services for the health insurance industry, I applied a simple methodology I had learned in strategy consulting with Booz Allen—go talk to people. So, I put together a list of about 50 different ideas, plus a dozen screens to help people visualize what I thought were the best ideas. Then I interviewed health insurance executives and asked them to rank these ideas on a scale of one to five—a "5" was a "must have," a "3" was a "nice to have," and a "1" meant no interest.

What I heard in response was exactly what strategy consultants tell executives in every industry. It's nice to have services that save administrative costs, provide competitive differentiation, or add value to an important constituent. Yet, everyone must have things to increase revenue and market share.

Just like the mantra "location, location, location" in real estate, the executives I met all told me that I would be welcomed into the boardrooms of health insurance companies if I had solutions to increase revenue and market share. This meant only two ideas from my list had potential for success—either use the Internet to enhance companies' existing distribution channels (health insurance brokers) or use the Internet to create a new channel.

Before embarking on this analysis, I thought I had executive support from my company to execute on my answer. In actuality, I had to fight passionately to get internal support for this new direction, even addressing the company at a lunchtime all-hands meeting by reciting Winston Churchill's wartime motto: "Never, never, never, never, never, never give up." Yet, as is often the case in any start-up, without a contract in hand for real revenue, the company could not invest in a new speculative idea.

Also, with an interim president trying to hire a permanent replacement at the time, there was no hope of pulling the trigger. I was committed to the idea, and only a few things could have kept me from leaving the company to pursue the idea on my own: a personal request from Jim Clark or John Doerr, a bribe of stock options, or my wife. Recognizing this, a Healtheon senior executive attempted to arrange a meeting for me with board member John Doerr, yet someone blocked the communication. So, neither John nor Jim knew I was leaving Healtheon to act on this business opportunity I had uncovered until after I had gone.

That situation turned out to be a huge blessing. In 1999, a year and a half later, we had over $1 million of revenue under our belt, we'd achieved a breakeven year, and we had funding offers from the Valley's top-tier VCs. At this point, Kleiner-Perkins, along with Weiss Peck and Greer, decided to back our Internet-based health insurance distribution start-up in a $12 million "series A" round.

### Who are your customers? Where are they from and what do they order?

Our customers vary widely. We have college grads looking for health insurance for themselves, small business owners with two to 50 employees shopping for an affordable health insurance plan for themselves and their employees, and families looking for a supplemental health plan for their elderly parents. And, because our services are available nationwide, we have customers from Florida to California and from all age groups.

People who become members of eHealthInsurance can buy health insurance plans that (1) provide the features and benefits they need, (2) meet the price point they can afford, and (3) deal with a leading health insurance carrier selling this type of plan in their home state.

## Looking back, what were some of the biggest obstacles facing the company in getting off the ground?

Licensing, licensing, licensing. We faced several significant crises in the process of obtaining and maintaining licenses to conduct business in 50 states. The process in each state required us to first obtain a health insurance sponsor, then obtain a state license, and then sign up the various health insurance companies in those states.

Although we thought we had our paperwork in line or the appropriate approvals from authorized representatives, we were sometimes blindsided or smothered by bureaucracy, which took us back to square one in certain states. Health insurance is a very complex business, as we quickly learned, and we continue to work to nurture our relationships with the departments of insurance in each state and the District of Columbia.

## What are some of the biggest victories that your company has achieved so far?

The greatest lasting victories were associated with maintaining both strategic focus and commitment to solid economic principles despite many pressures to do otherwise.

Although eHealthInsurance sounds narrow in its exclusive focus on health insurance, it is precisely this focus that has allowed us to obtain critical affiliate partnerships with other online financial services sites, such as General Electric's GEFN, which offers financial services and insurance, except for health.

Another example of focus is that we target only individuals and small businesses, which represent 90 percent of all businesses in the U.S., rather than mid- or large-sized businesses. Hence, we were able to strike business partnerships with some of the nation's largest health insurance brokers that were not equipped to handle the health insurance leads from small businesses. It was long-time mentor, advisory board member, and former director of Boston Consulting Group, Allen Phipps, who suggested that by focusing on becoming best-of-breed in a targeted area, the worst we could do was create real value.

My MBA training came from Wharton, where we were taught that everything is valued based on its ability to generate cash flow. From the very start, I was attracted to this business because of its solid economic model, including its ability to make more revenue per customer than the cost per customer.

While many companies were giving portals big chunks of their company and cash just to appear on their sites, we focused on win-win affiliate relationships as the source of most of our customers. A longtime friend, board member, and former marketing executive of AOL, Bob Lisbonne, suggested that we not only maintain focus, but also avoid "cash-ectomies," huge unjustified cash drains from portals. We still operate in this mode.

**If you had to do it all over again, what might you do differently to bring the business to where it is today?**

I have enormous respect and gratitude for those earliest friends and employees who invested the sweat, tears, and all-nighters to build this business. I wish I could have found ways to recognize and reward them more. Perhaps I still can!

I wish I could have sweated the administrative details less and invested more time on leadership to improve the customer's experience. The real problem was that I was CEO of a company employing 70-odd people, acting CFO, and VP of marketing—

all while simultaneously raising financing and ramping up the company nationwide. The solution would have been to hire for those key executive spots sooner.

**People reading about your start-up in this book might be inspired to start their own Internet-based company. What would you offer as advice?**

Before starting a business, ask the tough, hard questions about how your product or service adds value beyond what your target customer has today. If you're not building real value, you won't have a lasting business. In the case of eHealthInsurance, the distribution process of health insurance to the fragmented individual and small-business market was broken. In fact, of the 20 percent of Americans who do not have health insurance, most are self-employed or work for small businesses.

Brokers typically want to focus on larger businesses so they can make more money per sale. Therefore, service levels to individuals and small businesses were low. Using the Internet as a tool, eHealthInsurance has been able to bring big-company service levels to the individual and small business for the first time. We provide selection, price transparency, benefits comparisons, doctor directories, instant quotes, and the application itself right online.

For those who need to talk with a specialist, we have a call center staffed with an army of experts. We also provide customer advocacy to help our members who are not getting the attention they need once they purchase a health insurance plan. Until eHealthInsurance came along, none of this existed for people who don't get their insurance through a large employer or for small businesses that wanted to provide health insurance benefits to their employees.

**What's the atmosphere like at your offices? Do you have a dress code, water cooler, and so forth?**

This is a very comfortable company to work for and with. The people who work for eHealthInsurance are smart, proactive, innovative, and customer focused. The work environment is casual, yet fairly traditional. Our offices are open work spaces with low cubical walls, which provide some privacy while inviting teamwork and camaraderie. There really is no stated dress code, and while people dress for comfort, the majority of employees come to the office in business-casual attire.

As far as water coolers go, eHealthInsurance does have them, but there are other more significant gathering places for employees. Our cafe not only has bottled water available, but also sodas, sparkling water, juices, coffee, and tea as well as snacks, fruit, and quick-fix meals—all for free. This setup helps to maintain employee morale and to enhance employee productivity.

Behind our building there is a parking lot that is often transformed into an inline skate hockey rink or a basketball court. At many times of the day and night, one can find employees playing a quick game of table tennis or foosball as well. The company even has a basketball team that plays in a local league, with engineers, sales people, and executives playing side by side.

Once a month, the company hosts a staff lunch. Different cuisine is ordered in each time, and employees share the meal together in a casual atmosphere. This gives employees a chance to socialize with people who are not on their organizational team, sharing ideas, jokes, and stories.

Employees can feel at home when they are at the office, and it reflects positively on the work that they do. This is their company, and they know that by maintaining focus and working together, they will build a successful company that will be the leader in this market for years to come.

***Are there any particular leaders, books, or other business ventures that served as an inspiration to you?***

As mentioned earlier, the business leaders who both inspired and helped me were Jim Clark and John Doerr. As for books, I remember one venture capitalist from a top-tier firm coming to our home before his firm made the decision to invest in eHealthInsurance. He asked if I had ever heard of the book *Built to Last*, and my wife went into our bedroom to pull out our copy. *Built to Last* has inspired me to set "big, hairy, audacious goals (BHAGS)," as well as to articulate and model core values that build a foundation for a lasting organization.

Far above business leaders, the person who inspires me most is Jesus of Nazareth. He cared for the poor, the sick, and the lowly. From my perspective, this inspires me to focus on the low-income uninsured. Jesus also demonstrated courage, optimism, conviction, and many other qualities of leadership that can inspire anyone.

My family and I come from a Hindu background, but many of us have been attracted to learning about Jesus. In fact, my own interest in Jesus has led me to serve as a board member of JesusInstitute.org, which helps people of all cultural and spiritual backgrounds learn about the person of Jesus.

***Looking down the road, where do you think the Internet is going? And in light of this, where is your site going?***

The Internet is the infrastructure that will connect people anywhere at anytime for commerce, communications, and content, and its ubiquity will continue to grow.

Since starting eHealthInsurance, we discovered that 40 percent of those who apply for health insurance at eHealthInsurance.com come from the uninsured population. One out of five Americans do not have health insurance. We realized that eHealthInsurance was applying the most revolutionary new technology, the Internet, to one of America's most pressing social problems, the uninsured.

The Internet can empower people with knowledge, and that means more and more of America's uninsured population can overcome the barriers to such information as where to buy health insurance, what it costs, and what is right for them. Affording Internet access is still a barrier for many, but with government initiatives to help out, the combination will be powerful.

With the Internet and government assistance, I think that both my personal experience and my uncle's situation could have been avoided. Remember, he came from India to run a small motel business in Texas, and although he became a U.S. citizen, he did not purchase health insurance. When his stroke occurred, he needed to return to India just to afford the therapy. No U.S. citizen should experience that type of life disruption.

We at eHealthInsurance.com can make a difference in helping to solve the problems of the uninsured, and we are committed to maintaining our focus on health insurance. We'll just continue to make it easier for customers to purchase their health insurance and make the decisions that are right for them.

# eMarketer.com

. . . . . . . . . . . . . . . . . . . . . . . . . . . . . . . . . . . .

### *Information is power*

THERE'S AN UNSPOKEN power to the statistics, research reports, and information that has been compiled about the fascinating new avenue of life called the Internet. This is what Sam Alfstad discovered when he first began to build eMarketer from his traditional advertising agency.

Good information reduces risk, and the business risk of the dotcom arena is not taken lightly these days. It's easy to see where the demand for eMarketer's statistics and information comes from.

As time goes by, the business environment changes. Risks change, demand for information changes—and so does eMarketer's offerings of informational products. It's a great site, and if you haven't visited it yet, check it out.

Forresters, Gartners, and other market research companies rely on this type of statistical information to build their businesses. And that's what gave eMarketer the beginnings for an enterprise that has proved valuable to the business titans of today's Internet. Sam gave us his story of how his business came to be.

**Tell us about your firm and what we'll find when we visit your site.**

Because we bill eMarketer as "the world's leading provider of Internet statistics," it's not too surprising to find stats on our site. We provide numbers, charts, graphs, and articles on the latest news, studies, and research covering online business and demographics—all the facts and figures Web marketers need to make critical business decisions.

We have 13 eChannels covering the different business disciplines that make up the main e-commerce interests today, such as B2B, B2C, eMail Marketing, eAdvertising, eAsia, wireless, broadband, and so on. Each channel employs an analyst who stays on top of each particular area of interest, and they all write weekly articles plus comprehensive overview reports that are published twice a year. We also have community groups for each area—we call them eBoards—and the discussions there are not only informative, but also pretty lively.

Our newest information tool is the eStatDatabase. It has more than 100,000 data points concerning online business. There's really nothing like it anywhere in the world, online or off. For example, within seconds our users can find out how many women are shopping online in France, how many billion songs were traded on Napster during the last month, or what the eBook market will be in the year 2004—you name it. The eMarketer research team scours more than 350 news publications every day and sees virtually all the online research produced anywhere on the globe. Then, on the basis of that research, our editorial staff adds between 150 and 250 new or revised data points to the database every day.

Essentially, we want eMarketer readers to find the business information and numbers they need to do business online. So, we make sure they have access to the most comprehensive, up-to-date information available.

**Let's talk about you, now, and how you came to found this business.**

I'm an old ad guy. I worked in New York as a copywriter, then as a creative director in hard-nosed, package goods agencies on Madison Avenue. My clients included Colgate-Palmolive, M&M Mars, the U.S. Air Force, and AirFrance. I wrote, shot, and produced more than 1,000 TV commercials.

One day I walked out of my last "big agency" and started my own agency, The Alfstad Blank Group. We called it TAG, as in "tag." I didn't like the compartmentalization of big agencies or the hierarchies. Their structures seemed anti-creative to me. Clients often ended up paying more than they should have because the TV group didn't talk to the direct group, which didn't talk to the promotion group, which didn't talk to PR, and so on.

I thought everyone should work together, so at TAG we had a motto: "No walls, low walls." We did everything for our clients from strategy and product development to design and identity, from collateral to outdoor, and from print to radio and TV. We worked with Ziff-Davis on some of its early CD-ROM information products; with COMSAT, the satellite communications pioneer; and with Olsten Staffing, which at that time was the second-largest staffing firm in the world.

***How did the firm and its site come to be? Is there an interesting story behind your start-up?***

At TAG we covered all media for our clients, but one day in the mid-nineties we happened to look up and there was a "new media"—the Internet, websites—and everybody was buzzing about this new thing. Naturally, since it was our business, we got interested. We got online, we got browsers, and to get some experience in this new medium, we tried to talk our clients into letting us build corporate websites for them. But no one was too sure about that yet.

So we looked around like curious little cats. Most of the information sites online at that time were, well, techie. They told you how to program HTML and how to build networks and what a .gif was. But if you went out to eat, for instance, what you heard buzzing in people's conversations were remarks like, "Do you think anyone can make money on this Internet?" or "What's a banner? How does it work?"

In short, people were interested in marketing online, but no one seemed to know how. So we thought, "Hey, we know marketing. Let's put up a site about that."

We launched e-land.com (yes, you could still get addresses like that then) in the summer of 1996. At the time, it was a hobby for our agency, a learning experience, but it got us work, too. We did award-winning websites for Olsten and the professional printers, Linotype, and we also handled DLJdirect's early online campaign, among others. All at once we were buying and selling ads online. By working both sides of the fence, we probably learned the business of online marketing as fast as anyone out there.

After two years we changed our name to eMarketer to give people a better idea of what we were all about and to build up awareness among Web marketers. We worked with ClickZ, ChannelSeven, Advertising Age, and other early marketing and advertising information sites to establish the idea of online marketing.

In the latter part of 1998, though, we had to make a decision. Our Internet "hobby" was taking up too much time and resources. Either we had to close up the online experiment and get serious about the traditional ad business, or we needed to shut down the agency and go online all the way.

In the first week of January 1999, we called up all our agency clients and resigned their accounts. By April 1st, we were all Internet, and we were also profitable that first month.

**Where, when, and how did you first get the idea for your business?**

As part of growing the awareness of eMarketer and gathering information, we went to various industry events in the New York City area. One afternoon I was sitting at my computer and Geoff Ramsey, one of the cofounders of eMarketer, came back from a luncheon seminar uptown. He was beaming, saying: "I got it, I got it, I got it."

"What have you got?" I asked.

"Give me a day and I'll show you," he said.

What he had come up with was the idea of aggregating data in much the same way that we were aggregating articles. That may sound dumb, but at the time hardly anyone was doing it, and no one was doing it on a regular basis.

You have to remember, it was the "early days" online, and everyone was asking questions such as, "How many people are online?" or, "How often do people go online and for how long?" There were answers to these questions, and research firms were looking into these issues, but the problem was that the figures they were coming up with were all over the cyberlot. One researcher would say a million this, while another would claim 50 million that. There was no consistency and a lot of confusion.

Geoff's idea was to gather all the figures and findings on a particular question and put them all together in one place, so it would be easy for businesspeople to compare them. At a glance, our readers could see what Forrester said, what Jupiter said, what Nielsen said, and what all the major researchers said on a given question.

Having this comparative data on hand all in one place was a great new business information tool, and the response was immediate. By phone, email, and in person, our readers told us how much they appreciated this new service. But . . . almost everyone followed the praise with the same question: "What does it all mean?"

So, we began looking into the numbers, separating apples from oranges, in order to understand why the numbers differed, and we refined eMarketer's mission statement to: "Aggregate, filter, organize, and analyze."

That simple "what does it all mean" led us to create a full-time team of fourteen analysts and report writers, five researchers, and six data entry people, plus four editors and a proofreader—all headed by Geoff Ramsey, who is now our "statsmaster."

The eMarketer website now sells millions of dollars of online information every year. Hundreds of thousands of Web marketers from around the world visit our site and receive our newsletters every month for the latest e-business news and numbers.

**Tell us some more about your customers. Are they individuals? Businesses? What do they order?**

In a recent article in the *Financial Times*, "Why B2B Is the Place to Be," Nich Bertolotti, head of European media research at JP Morgan, said, "Businesses are used to subscribing. They are used to paying for things. When they move onto the Internet, they keep paying." This statement sums up eMarketer's targeting and product-building philosophies.

So our customers are businesspeople from both large and small businesses all over the world, especially managers and others in charge of developing corporate Internet initiatives. These individuals are overwhelmingly from the ranks of upper-middle and senior management, with job titles such as CEO, president, managing director, COO, CFO, CTO/CIO, CMO, VP of marketing, VP of business development, director of research, corporate librarian, and analyst.

Geographically, the U.S. is our largest single market, and we expect that will continue to be the case. But we also expect significant growth in Europe and the Asia/Pacific region. We have recently opened an office in Tokyo and have negotiated a reseller agreement with Japan's largest research sales company, JMAR. We are also negotiating reseller agreements in Europe.

The various geographic markets (in order) that eMarketer is currently targeting are:

- U.S. and Canada
- Japan (followed by Korea and China)
- Europe (probably centered on U.K. and Germany)
- South America
- the rest of the world (led by India and Australia)

We project that Japan will account for approximately 8 percent of sales next year and Europe about 20 percent. In the long term, we expect Europe and Asia/Pacific will each account for 30 percent of sales.

**Looking back, what were some of the biggest obstacles facing the company in getting off the ground?**

In the beginning, we didn't know we had a business. We were putting in tremendously long hours and one hell of a lot of effort on learning. This was before the dot-com stock boom, so most people we knew thought we were crazy.

Once we decided to close the agency and become an Internet information company, things got clearer. Because eMarketer bootstrapped its own growth, we concentrated on building the business and staying profitable. It was a tough haul sometimes, and maybe we didn't grow as fast as we could have. In hindsight, though, after the dot-com bust, it may have been a blessing in disguise.

**What have been some of the biggest victories you've experienced in taking the site to where it is?**

We are happy to be surviving and thriving in the current economy. At eMarketer, we don't think in terms of victories or defeats, and we shy away from the old economy's business-as-war mentality. Rather than thinking in terms of competition, we concentrate on cooperating with the companies in the space around us.

For example, we provide content for publishers that also aggregate content, such as Business 2.0, EUI, Entrepreneur, CNN MoneyLine, and TechTV—in fact, hundreds of news outlets. In return, they help raise our profile in the business communities they serve. We also take content from research companies and consultancies, but then promote their expertise and services to the business-service buyers they wish to reach. So, we all work together.

***If you had to do it all over again, are there things you would do differently to bring the business where it is today?***

One thing, I think I should have grown eMarketer faster by going out and taking investment capital sooner. As CEO, I showed an ignorance of financial marketers and how to use the opportunities they provided.

***Many people in this world have a passion for a business of their own. For someone wanting to start an Internet company, what could you offer as advice?***

There are two things an Internet entrepreneur must never forget:

> (1) Don't make the mistake of thinking an Internet business is different from other businesses. Fundamental rules apply.

> (2) Always remember that an Internet business is fundamentally different from other businesses. You can't play by the old rules and win.

Yes, these are contradictions, but both statements are true. Any businessperson who tries to ignore either of them is going to fail online.

### If I were a fly on the wall in your offices, what would I see? Do you have a normal office with a dress code and water coolers?

Controlled chaos. No spas, gyms, basketball courts, or any of the new economy trappings, but the office is completely open—no walls, time clocks, cubicles, or dress codes. At eMarketer, we hire adults. We want people who are excited about their work and about growing eMarketer into a worldwide brand.

### Are there any individuals, books, or other business ventures that have served as inspirational models for your business?

The book that inspired me throughout the time that we were building eMarketer was *Competing for the Future*, published in 1994 by Gary Hamel and C.K. Prahalad. They stressed that winning in business was not about being number one, but about "who gets to the future first." They urged companies to create their own futures, to envision new markets, and to reinvent themselves—and that's exactly what we did. I would recommend this book to anyone who is seriously considering starting or building a business, whether online or off.

### Where do you see the Internet going, and, in light of this, where do you see your site going?

The business user, B2B, is eMarketer's target, and the growth in this segment is being driven by factors other than the stock market. The need to stay competitive, drive down costs, open new markets, and take advantage of emerging procurement and communications systems are the diverse business imperatives that will fuel growth for years to come in the U.S. In Europe and the Asia/Pacific arena, Internet business growth cycles have only just begun.

Steve Butler, eMarketer's B2B analyst, projects that worldwide B2B e-commerce will grow from $124 billion in 2000 to $747 billion in 2003. Including B2C revenues, total online commerce is projected to be $851 billion (B2C businesses need information, too). By any measure, that constitutes huge and rapid growth. In order to develop, large and small businesses around the world are obviously going to need continuous access to information and data about the Internet.

The catch phrase "the Internet is everywhere" has not even begun to be true, but it will be. You ain't seen nuthin' yet!

# 14

# E-Poll.com

## A portal of expression

ALL TRUE-BLUE BOOTSTRAPPERS will be inspired as they listen to Gerry Phillpott's account of breaking into the world of network television: "I didn't know anyone and had nowhere to stay, but I managed to find a rundown student hotel and convinced a few people at the networks to meet with me."

Hear a little more of Gerry's story, and you'll hone in on a line that describes someone with a dream, but a savvy dream: "I've always been a gambler, but have spent no more than $100 total in Vegas."

Careful, but adventurous, Gerry has created a great business entity called E-Poll.com. It thrives on the fundamentally American maxims that we're all entitled to our opinion and what we think matters. Gerry's efforts have been admirable, and here's his spin on the what, where, why, when, and how of E-Poll.

**Can you tell us about your firm and what can be found on your site?**

Offering interactive services for television, wireless and the Web, E-Poll.com is a leading content enabler with polling software (ASP), innovative market research, advertising services, syndicated content, and an extensive database of viewer profiles and preferences. E-Poll.com offers a new distribution system for helping clients target and reach their specific customers.

The fact is, with thousands of Internet, broadband, and wireless companies competing for customers, gathering intelligent data for building revenues is extremely critical. Whether a business is based on advertising or e-commerce, E-Poll.com's technology, database of members, and advertising tools offer a vital one-stop solution for businesses wanting to move forward.

They'll find a site where anyone can come in and express themselves on issues from news and politics to lifestyles and entertainment. Our goal is to become "the portal of expression," a term coined by one of our clients.

### Can you give us some background about yourself and how you came to found this business?

From 1987 to 1997, I was vice president of sales for Multimedia Entertainment in Los Angeles. There, I was responsible for the creation, direction, and execution of sales and marketing plans for one of the leading syndication companies in the industry. I oversaw the distribution of shows as varied as Donahue, Sally Jessy Raphael, Rush Limbaugh, and Young People's Specials, among others.

Prior to that, I was director of affiliate relations for the ABC Television Network in New York. While there, I designed campaigns for marketing and promoting ABC shows and negotiated programming commitments with the network's affiliates. I also coordinated the ABC News exit poll data for the affiliates during the 1980 and 1984 presidential election coverage.

In the San Francisco market, I spent some time as the creative director for KICU-TV, where I developed station image campaigns, sales promotions, and scheduled programs.

I've always been a gambler, but I've spent no more than $100 total in Vegas. I sold everything I had and left college three months before graduation to find a job in New York at one of the networks. (I later got my degree after completing some course work.) I didn't know anyone in the city and had nowhere to stay, but I managed to find a rundown student hotel.

Then, I was able to convince a few people at the networks to meet with me. After five weeks of looking for work and almost no money left, I got calls from NBC, CBS, and ABC all on the same day—May 19, 1979. That was the moment that I knew gambles can pay off.

I worked for ABC for awhile, but I didn't like the direction my department was taking. I also wanted a change, so I quit a very good job to move back to Los Angeles to be more entertainment focused. That caught the attention of a gambler himself, Tom Shannon at Multimedia, and he made me the head of sales for its first-run products, such as Donahue, Sally Jessy Raphael, and Jerry Springer, to name a few.

This was a time of massive consolidation within the industry, and in late 1996 Multimedia was sold to then Universal, now StudiosUSA. I was offered great opportunities to stay in syndication, but I chose to quit and stay home for the birth of my first child. At that point, my ongoing passion about new media and the potential for true interactivity came out, and I formed Bridge Entertainment. The name was a rather obvious metaphor for my idea of helping traditional media bridge the gap to new media.

Out of that concept—the idea of surveying people's needs and offering the visceral opportunity to sound off—E-Poll was born. There were no sites I could find in late 1996 or early 1997 that offered an aggregated gateway for expressing opinions. Yes, there were chat, forums, and self-publishing, but no one place offered people from all walks of life a chance to get involved. I wanted E-Poll to be that place.

*How did the firm and its site come to be? Is there an interesting story behind your start-up?*

I always remember the great scene in Paddy Chayefsky's *Network* in which Peter Finch rallied everyone to proclaim, "I'm mad as hell, and I'm not going to take it any more." However, with television being a one-way medium, there was no way to poll people's opinions. I actually woke up in the middle of the night with the idea for E-Poll. I immediately called Earthlink, got a domain name and a little website in a matter of 15 minutes, and then went back to bed. I later found out the trademark was available (I guess I should have checked that first) and then proceeded to lock down the trademark. We were in business.

*Do you recall how, when, or where you first started thinking of the idea for this business?*

The reason to start the business came into play as I saw the need to get immediate data in a reliable, cost-effective, and efficient way. Venting is great, but it doesn't necessarily pay the bills. I saw that the Internet (as well as interactive TV and wireless PDAs) was going to revolutionize the way we learn about our customers and view trends. Plus, it would give disparate groups of people the ability to interact with one another and compare and contrast how they view life.

Traditional research was a $5 billion market, and yet a good two-thirds of the business community couldn't afford real access to research on consumer trends. More specifically, they couldn't even afford to survey their own customers beyond the cursory information gleaned from rudimentary "reply cards." We were able to develop a technology that helped level the playing field, where large and small businesses could get the critical information they needed to thrive competitively in the marketplace.

*Can you tell us about some of your customers? Where are they from and what do they order?*

I come from 20-plus years in the entertainment industry, and one thing I learned in those years is that this business is definitely pervasive. Establishing your brand within this industry, even something as boring as Nielsen, will get people to know your name. If Joe Public knows who you are, you can be assured that current and future clients will know you are a player. Therefore, my first line of attack was the entertainment client base for the reason I just stated, and also because I knew most of the players and they knew I understood their needs.

My initial intention was that advertisers would support a good portion of the website, but within a few weeks of launching it in October 1997, the bottom fell out of the online ad market for sites outside of the top 100. Obviously, I had to rethink my strategy.

In the meantime, we had people signing up to take polls and earn points. E-Poll.com and MyPoints.com were among the very first points programs online, and we saw that we could get immediate feedback through our panel. I have a degree in psychology, which made me knowledgeable about statistics and sampling, and I was careful to weigh and monitor our early samples. Even so, I found the results we were delivering to our clients were lining up very nicely with "traditional" research results that they were getting through tracking studies.

Our first two major clients were Rysher (now part of Paramount), which we did market research for, and NBC, which asked us to develop our polling technology for use on its Interactive Neighborhood. More than 80 local NBC affiliates joined the NBC IN as a consortium.

As we developed and refined our products, services, and technology, our clients included CBS, AFI, Disney, NATPE, Columbia TriStar Interactive, and Microsoft TV, among others. These companies have licensed our technology, which allows them to survey their own customers, as well as tap into our database of members to get a "snapshot" of opinions on TV shows, pilots, new products, or trends in the industry.

**_Looking back, what were some of the biggest obstacles facing the company in getting off the ground?_**

The biggest obstacle was starting the company with "me, myself, and I." While there has been incredible support from friends, family, and peers in the industry who have consulted, advised, invested, and helped out, I didn't have the team that many of the new media companies started with. It was a very personal dream, and I just didn't have the relationships on the tech side, nor did I have the "fools" that sometimes quit their job and join you in your dream.

The second biggest obstacle was owning a company that was not particularly flashy in a community that made a company such as DEN a virtual sex symbol. No investor would get someone "oohing" and "aahing" at a cocktail party in Los Angeles or San Francisco by telling them he or she invested in an online research company. DEN and other sexy content plays, along with anything that smelled like e-commerce, were the hot companies, and they were getting all the so-called smart money players falling over each other to get in. Immediate availability to valuable information was viewed as a "small play," so our access to venture funds was limited. We had to survive on limited revenues and a very tight fiscal plan. What a concept.

These two challenges made it more difficult to grow the company at the pace I felt was needed to take advantage of our early entry into online research. Eventually, Harris and CyberDialogue's offline research division, along with a few others, began to enter this market, and they had the financing to grab a share.

**_What have been some of the biggest victories you've experienced in taking the site to where it is?_**

With every challenge, there are opportunities. We had an early victory when I established a relationship with the VP of NBC Interactive, Vinnie Grosso, who knew me from my traditional broadcast days. He wanted me to design the interactive polling module for the NBC stations. His review of other polling software and technology companies then showed that they just didn't understand the unique needs of the entertainment community. We did.

We were able to develop a turnkey polling technology that local broadcasters, networks, and entertainment companies could use on their websites. Features such as the ability to suppress results so they could tease on-air programming, instantaneous access during live broadcasts, and a number of other functionality requirements gave us a competitive advantage over what was on the street.

With NBC as a client on the technology side and with a few key projects that we won from Rysher, Pearson Television, and CBS, we were immediately put in the running as a contender in the information and data-gathering business.

Another victory was when w aligned with the trade organization NATPE (National Association of Television Program Executives), which sponsors the largest programming conference in the world. All 3,000 of its member companies are potential clients of E-Poll, and having the platform and credibility that comes with such an organization allowed us to develop our base of clients

Lastly, the downturn of the market in April 2000 led to forecasts of the death of many start-ups. But, while the "big play" companies were no longer getting hard looks from investors, the infrastructure and B2B enablers that had some traction as smaller operations were now becoming more attractive as the ensuing correction in the market took place. Therefore, as we met with potential clients and partners in the spring of 2000, what started as talks to work together became talks about investing. I was fortunate to have already started a relationship with Sam Alfstad of eMarketer, where we both believed there was great synergy between our two companies.

Unbeknownst to me, at that time Sam was forming a venture group/incubator (B2B-Hive, LLC) with his partners, and that ultimately led to our raising capital in July of 2000. They had the belief that incubators, if developed correctly, could be a viable business and were necessary during this churn period to offer stability, consistency, and critical levels of support to their investment companies.

Of course, the biggest victory, if you will—asset is the right word—is an incredibly supportive family that allowed me to spend better than three years as an entrepreneur without a safety net.

### Is there anything you would have do differently if you could start the business all over again?

Share the wealth and share the misery—that is what I would do over again. Not that I was greedy early on, but the people I wanted to bring on board as early partners just didn't have the passion I did for this business plan. They had their own dreams that they were chasing. Instead of searching around more and looking outside my sphere of influence for partners, I just seized the opportunity that was available and built it myself.

I didn't have relationships at that time at the university level. In hindsight, it would have been worth the time to nurture such relationships and perhaps find those people who both shared my vision and could immediately bring their academic and technology prowess to our model.

Keep in mind that in those days the mantras were "speed to market" and "fail fast." My concern was that taking extra time and not jumping immediately on the opportunity to build out my website would put me at a competitive disadvantage. Of course, not having the money and the team to build my dream had the same negative impact.

**No business start-up is easy, so what kind of advice would you offer to someone wanting to start an Internet business?**

Get used to hearing "no." When you spend 20 years on the sales and marketing side of the entertainment business as I have, you get used to hearing that word. I had to say it myself when I worked on the program development side of the business. But, make that word your friend because you'll hear it 15 times for every time you hear "yes" once. If your plan is good and your passion is high, though, you might be able to lower that ratio.

"Selling starts with no," as the old saying goes. Knowing this prepares you for the incredible highs and lows that come with running your own business. You also learn that it will take time to get your message across to the right people, so be sure to allow for that. Overcoming objections and rejection, refining your vision, staying focused, and maintaining a belief in yourself will only make you more resolved to continue. If it doesn't, then that should be a clear signal you either need a partner who can handle this or that starting your own company is not the best idea.

**What is your workplace environment like? Do you have a normal business office?**

Sorry to say, it is pretty much business as usual from the standpoint of normal offices. Just the usual desks, chairs, water coolers, and dress codes. No pets, massage rooms, oxygen tents, or any of that fun stuff around here.

**Many business ventures are inspired by great leaders or other business start-up stories. What books, individuals, or other ventures served as models for your business?**

There were no real inspirational leaders that I read or heard about on the business side that I can point to. However, my parents, who were risk takers, and other mentors and old bosses were the most influential and inspirational. Also, hearing war stories from other start-ups were helpful.

I remember Bob Turner, former president of Multimedia Entertainment, inspiring me with his stories of starting up his entertainment companies and the risks and rewards that came with that. He also advised me to start and build my business while I was trying to raise money. While that was counterintuitive at the time, it proved out to be my savior as the investment market began to rethink the new technologies.

**Looking down the road, where is the Internet going and how will your site be affected?**

I've always seen the Internet as one component of many that we were going to operate within. It offered a very low barrier to entry as we started our business in 1997, but I've always had the Internet, kiosks, wireless, PDAs, GPS devices, and interactive television in our business plan as additional platforms that we would publish across. You hear the terms "anytime, anywhere" often these days, and that is consistent with our goal to provide interactive opportunities for viewers and consumers, and for our clients.

The Internet is and will continue to be a dominant player in our business plan and in our future success. I think that the strengths of the Internet—information gathering, email, research, some commerce, and community—are also our strengths, so E-Poll.com's products and services will continue to be extremely compatible with the Internet of the future.

# 15

# Experience.com

*Building experience is in itself an experience*

AT LEAST JENNIFER FLOREN thinks so. When most of her peers were finishing grad school, chasing members of the opposite sex, and starting to get early jitters about their first or second job out of college, Jennifer got a bug bite. The entrepreneurial bug, that is.

The Ivy League graduate didn't talk about being her own boss. She didn't spout it as a "someday I'd like to" pipe dream. She did it, and she did it at 26 years of age!

At Dartmouth and virtually every other institution of higher learning, students are taught to write about what they know. With this principle in mind, Jennifer set out to start a business around something she knew—the job market for freshly minted college graduates.

"Armed with a hope, a prayer, and some good feedback, I resigned from Bain to become a full-time entrepreneur," says Jennifer. It makes you want to wave the American flag and hope that your son and daughter have the same courage and heartfelt zeal. Learn more about her story in the pages that follow.

**Tell us about your company and what a visitor to your website will find.**

As the leader in the college student and alumni "e-cruiting" market, Experience.com is revolutionizing the way employers attract and retain young talent, as well as the way students and alumni transition into the working world. My company works with thousands of employers, more than 350 universities nationwide, and more than two million students and alumni to create a better employment match for both the candidate and the employer.

We have a hugely successful print magazine, *Experience*, with a circulation of more than one million college students and young professionals nationwide. We also provide a Web-based recruiting solution, eRecruiting, which helps university career centers automate the on-campus recruiting process.

There are two main groups of visitors to our site: (1) college students and/or young professionals and (2) employers. When a college student or young professional comes to our site, he or she has access to unique content and job postings targeted specifically at entry-level candidates. When an employer visits our site, it has access to millions of prequalified candidates.

### How does your site generate revenue?

Currently, there are four sources of revenue:

- fees paid by employers to post jobs on our site
- fees paid by universities for our eRecruiting solution
- online advertising
- magazine advertising

### Can you give us an overview of how you started the company? What challenges and lessons were significant on your entrepreneurial journey?

After I graduated from Dartmouth College in the early 1990s, I started working at Bain & Company as a management consultant. I thought this was going to be my dream job. I'd get to work at a top-tier firm that would pay me to solve interesting problems, work with great people, and see lots of companies up close.

Three years later, I wasn't so sure that this was my dream job. Bain's people were fantastic and the opportunity to learn about lots of companies was real, but I had a growing sense of uneasiness about calling myself a consultant all my life. Consulting was a job for me, but not a passion.

At the same time, my panicked younger sister was calling me from college on a daily basis. She was about to graduate and had no idea what to do with her life. That's when the entrepreneurial bug bit me.

As I listened to her, understood her anxiety, and looked at my own career's lack of direction, I realized that millions of ambitious young people like myself and my sister were in the same position. All of us were unsure of how to launch our careers and find our true paths in life. So, I decided to try to reinvent how college students approach their careers and somehow turn my passion into a viable business.

If I really wanted to reinvent how college students approach their careers, I needed a plan. I'm young, but my definition of a viable business is positively old-fashioned. That is, a unique idea that customers will pay for, that can be profitably delivered, and that your competitors can't copy overnight. I'd seen many clients at Bain stumble on these concepts, and I knew it wasn't going to be easy for me to get there.

From this experience comes my first piece of advice. You'll get nowhere without proving that you've solved the riddle of the basic business model. Working at night and on weekends, I did the homework that helped me transform my dream into what I call my core beliefs and, eventually, into a real business plan. Core beliefs are the building blocks of any business plan. They describe how you see the world differently from other people.

For me, core beliefs include: (1) understanding that students are unique in how they view and plan their careers, (2) treating university career centers as partners (not obstacles) in helping students, (3) knowing that educating candidates is as important as providing job postings, and (4) realizing that employers are an integral part of the solution, not an afterthought.

Here's some more advice. If you have no core beliefs about your business idea or if you can't put them into words, go back to the drawing board.

My first drafts of a business plan fell way short of the mark, but I ultimately honed an idea that I could share with a close circle of friends, many of whom became investors later. Armed with a hope, a prayer, and some good feedback, I resigned from Bain and became a full-time entrepreneur.

Those may have been the "go-go" days for some Internet start-ups, but life for me was far from glamorous. I worked alone from my apartment for almost six months with a printer/fax/copier that practically cooked dinner for me before I finally found office space. I spent this time refining my business model and laying the groundwork for what would become *Experience* magazine and its sister job-posting and career resource website, www.experience.com.

The business concept at the end of this long road was a model of simplicity—collaborate with career centers at top schools to bring employers and advertisers together with students and alumni in a fun, learning environment. Then, charge employers and advertisers for access to this audience so that it can be a free resource for students and career centers.

More free advice. If your friends and parents can't describe what your business does or how you'll stay afloat, keep simplifying your plans until they're shorter and sweeter than you ever thought possible.

Looking back, the early days of launching our magazine and website are a blur of late nights, endless details, and lots of laughs. I learned that it's important to have fun along the way and to make time to celebrate your team's successes. Laughter is important because the worrying always seems to take care of itself! My heart skips every time I think of how many people our company reaches—students and employers alike. Three years ago, I would have laughed if you'd told me we'd be working with hundreds of schools, thousands of employers, and millions of students and alumni.

The balance between an entrepreneur's passion and the need to be hard-nosed is a delicate one. Err too far on one side, and you have nothing more than an unpaid hobby. But err too far on the other, and you have a passionless job that will drain you physically and emotionally. When people ask me, I tell them I feel lucky to believe so passionately in what I'm doing. My new dream job? That's easy. I'm living it every day. It's one where I can do well as a businessperson while knowing that I'm also doing some good in the world. If your passion is like mine and drives you to a workable business plan, go for it. You'll be well on your way to happiness and success.

**No business start-up is easy, but, like yourself, many people have a passion for a business of their own. What do you think is the best way to start?**

Dream big, but don't believe that entrepreneurial success comes from anything but persistence and hard work! Your small victories eventually add up to weekly and monthly progress. If you're lucky, that progress gets your business one step closer to success. It's not always glamorous, but this is the success staircase that moves you from fanciful idea to booming business.

Start with a dream, and hone it into a viable business idea. Them, get the concept funded with seed money to prove the concept. Next, expand the company with a larger team and more external funding. The path's less clear beyond this point, but most entre-preneurs look for ways of at least partially cashing out to reward their investors and team. Simple, right?

I remember those first few months as being some of the best in my life. The reality, of course, was filled with equal parts exhila-ration, frustration, and anxiety. It was fun to solve problems, make decisions, and get things done. The progress was incre-mental, but eventually I was able to look back and see some accomplishments.

Real frustration came from my own style of always wanting to do more, only faster and better. Back then, I had no patience for an afternoon spent shopping for a new fax machine, even if it was the company's biggest cash outlay for the week. I never wor-ried about making money, but my anxiety arose when I paused to reflect on our mission. Reinventing the job search process for a few million people can sometimes feel like a daunting task!

Goals and discipline are everything in the unstructured early days of a start-up. I gave myself a year to get through this "prove you have a business" stage and accomplish what I called my ten mile-stones for success. Broadly, success meant proving the key ele-ments of my concept, but my milestones served to break down my goal into a short list of things that really mattered.

Milestones are different for every entrepreneur, but for me they were things like building my team, developing a magazine pro-totype, designing a concept for our website, attracting investors, and developing my business skills. If I wasn't progressing toward my milestones, I knew I was wasting time. My advice to aspiring entrepreneurs is to focus on what really matters. It's never a long list, but the temptation to stray is unbelievably strong.

*You've certainly been generous with your advice. Any other tips you'd like to share about getting through the early stages of a start-up?*

Sure, there's lots. First of all, though, be money smart. Entrepreneurs run out of money before they run out of ideas, so be thoughtful about tapping your savings and your network of family and friends. Figure out how much you think you'll need, then get your hands on at least 50 percent more than that.

Loans or investments can be the right answer, but that will depend on your situation. You'll want to consider both options, though it may be too early for most venture capitalists. However, you could find success with those who specialize in seed money and early-stage financing.

Regardless of your personal habits, develop a revenue and expense budget for your company and ration every nickel as if it were your last. Money in the bank is your only guarantee that you'll be around next week. Lastly, watch for creeping overhead expenses that can drain your cash. I worked from my living room and took no salary for longer than I care to remember.

As far as people go, you'll need a team. In fact, team building ranks with fundraising as the top preoccupation of most entrepreneurs. Hire quickly, but get the right people, meaning you'll want to hire based on your needs and your own weaknesses so that you can fill talent gaps. In the early days, be prepared to hire a less-experienced team than you'd otherwise prefer. Seasoned talent usually avoids early-stage companies and can be quite expensive anyway. If you can land one or two veterans for your most critical gaps, you'll have done very well.

Also, be visible with the right people. Low-cost, grassroots efforts are the key to visibility with potential customers, employees, and investors. At Experienc.com, we've done it all. We've given speeches, issued press releases, applied for awards, attended conferences, cold-called prospects, written articles, and posted to online discussion groups. Occasional publicity breakthroughs contributed immensely to our company's momentum and legitimized our business in the eyes of a lot of people.

Building a network of mentors is also a very important component. Even leaders need a sounding board. You'll want to develop a group of trusted confidants with whom you can seek advice, test an idea, or just gripe about a problem.

Spouses and loved ones can play this role, but it gets old for them pretty quickly. A better idea might be an informal group consisting of parents, family friends, neighbors, classmates, professors from school, personal friends, fellow entrepreneurs, and even select customers.

Lastly, be your own best salesperson. If you won't proudly sell your product or service, nobody else will. For me, the key was developing our business with a real sense as to what employers, students, and career centers needed. Knowing their worlds inside out, I'm convinced we have great tools that they need—somebody like me just needs to tell them! Selling is easy with this mentality.

The entrepreneurial success staircase is a series of tests. If you pass the tests, you'll eventually get the nod to progress to the next level. Each level brings new opportunities and challenges for you and your team, but turning a dream into a plan is the first step. Building a business around your plan and proving its feasibility is the next. Pass those tests, and you'll be challenged to play for keeps by scaling your business with serious venture capital backing and a team of professionals.

**What's the atmosphere like in your business offices? Do you have a dress code, break room, and so forth?**

The phrase "click and mortar" comes to mind when I think of our offices. We're located in an old historic building right in the heart of Boston at the Faneuil Hall Marketplace, which is well known for its history, tourism, restaurants, and retail shops. When we moved in, we knocked down as many walls as possible to open up the space so as to enhance internal communications and collaboration. Then, we brightened up the walls with very modern colors—shades of oranges, greens, and bright blues. Now, we're actually a blend of cool, Internet start-up and traditional brick.

The office atmosphere reflects our employees, I think—bright, funky, colorful, and hip. As of October 2000, we have approximately 100 employees working in a very fast-paced environment. There's no official dress code. Jeans and sneakers are quite common, though we do have the traditional water coolers. We also enjoy a few happy hours as a company. Lots of work, but lots of fun!

### Looking ahead, where do you see the Internet going, and how will Experience.com be affected?

As far as technology is concerned, I think we'll be seeing a huge increase in broadband. With lots more bandwidth, we'll see faster downloads, more audio/video, and a general improvement in performance—faster and cheaper than ever. I also think that mobile computing is going to explode. The Palm Pilot is just the beginning.

I think a general Internet business trend will be less funding for weak ideas. We've already seen this in the volatile tech market over the last few months. Basically, it'll be a huge shakeout where the clear Internet winners will get bigger and the losers will just fade away.

At Experience.com, we're going to focus on creating even cooler features that will result in a better matching of people and jobs. These can include artificial intelligence, search robots, searching, matching, and the like, as well as multimedia features, such as videoconferencing and streaming video. Maybe even some mobility features, such as getting paged with job offers! Finally, I do expect us to dominate our niche.

*By trying, we can
easily learn to endure adversity
—another man's, I mean.*

*— Mark Twain*

# 16

# FeedRoom.com

. . . . . . . . . . . . . . . . . . . . . . . . . . . . . . . . . . . . .

### *TV away from TV*

JON KLEIN IS A COLORFUL character who has created a colorful business. Basically, the FeedRoom is TV away from TV. Jon got the idea in the control room of a major network during the Gulf War and, well . . . today we have FeedRoom.com.

If there's ever a story about guts and courage, it seems that Jon Klein has displayed it. As Klein says, make sure you have "an ego big enough so that when it gets whittled away, you've still got something left." It seems Klein has lived his philosophy. He left his high-flying New York TV network job to become an entre-preneur and created a business that feeds on a gap he saw in his TV control room experience. Here's how Jon describes it.

**When we visit the FeedRoom, what will we find?**

Lots! Visit our website, and you'll find the biggest video player you've ever seen on your computer showing the latest news from NBC, CBS, Tribune, and a host of other name-brand providers. The FeedRoom is a broadband news network that offers viewers the chance to watch local, national, or international news and information—even if they're away from a TV.

**Tell us a something about your background and how you came to found this business.**

As executive vice president of CBS news, I was responsible for overseeing *60 Minutes* and the rest of the prime-time programming. I had always heard tales of what fun the pioneers of television had while inventing this brand-new medium, so when broadband came along, I seized the chance to have a little more fun myself.

**How did the firm and its site come to be? Is there an interesting story behind your start-up?**

Well, first I upped and quit my job, leaving lots of soon-to-be-valuable stock options behind. After that, I moved from a corner suite with a river view to a fifth floor walk-up in the garment district that I cadged off a friend, and then I spent six months going walkabout, attending conferences and reading everything I could get my hands on.

Once I was satisfied that no one was doing anything like what I had in mind, I went ahead and wrote a business plan that played to my strengths as an Emmy and Peabody award-winning journalist. I know how to tell stories using video, and I was sure that media companies could do a better job telling stories online by using rich media—which plays to their strengths in video—as opposed to text-heavy narrowband websites.

I then went to my former CEO, Peter Lund, and was able to win his support and investment. With that as validation, I contacted an old friend who's now president of a VC firm and got his commitment for funding. Then I went to a former colleague who was running an Internet incubator and got him on board. With these people in hand, I was able to approach Intel and get its participation. Now, we had enough to get started.

I have always relied on a network of friends and colleagues—people I know, trust, and whose opinions I respect—rather than total strangers. For example, one of my senior managers went to junior high school with me; another went to college with me;

and one of our original investors is the head of investment banking for UBS Warburg. Working within your own network saves a lot of communication time, and it builds trust within the new enterprise..

**Where, when, and how did you first get the idea for your business?**

I was sitting in a control room at CBS News during the Gulf War looking at the array of video monitors in front of me. Each monitor was supplied by a satellite feed from a different part of the world, and I thought how cool it would be for viewers to be able to watch the war this way, in the raw, choosing which feed to punch up instead of relying on the producers to select for them. I kept that thought in the back of my mind, just waiting for the technology to make it possible, and as soon as it was, I leapt.

**Can you tell us about some of your customers? Are they individuals? Businesses?**

Our customers are major media companies, such as NBC, CBS, and Tribune. They work with us to bring their product, video information, into a broadband offering in the form of co-branded local "FeedRooms"—the NBC San Diego FeedRoom, for example—which are consumer destination websites. Now, we are also beginning to work with them on back office solutions using the broadband Web to help them sell advertising and distribute promotional materials.

Then we have viewers, who are the ultimate customers. They use us to stay in touch with what's going in the world in a form they prefer—watching, instead of reading, information.

**What were some of the biggest obstacles your company faced in getting off the ground?**

The biggest obstacle was convincing media companies that they needed to be in broadband. They all turned a deaf ear until the AOL/Time Warner merger, which suddenly put "convergence strategy" on everyone's lips. The fact that no one had such a strategy was very helpful for us.

**What are some of the biggest successes you've experienced in taking the site to where it is today?**

Probably the biggest success was getting my wife to agree to let me quit one of the greatest jobs in the world and try this crazy idea. Also, the NBC, CBS, and Tribune deals put us on the map and gave us a chance to show how we can add value to well-established, Fortune 500 companies.

**If you had to do it all over again, what, if anything, would you do differently?**

I would commit to expensive office space sooner. We will be moving next month, and we're ecstatic to finally be in one location together. Up to now, sales and marketing have been spread out over several locations. The new space isn't lavish or anything, but I hate having that big rent bill hanging over my head every month. It feels like when I first moved to New York City at age 24 and committed to a studio apartment, which meant I had to eat tuna seven days a week.

**So many people yearn to have a business of their own. For someone wanting to start an Internet company, what could you offer as advice?**

First off, make sure you've got an ego big enough so that when it gets whittled away, you've still got something left. It's extraordinary to what degree an entrepreneur must stand with his feet firmly planted in the ground, sticking to his vision when absolutely no one else agrees. Also, before you make the leap, make sure you've got a network of friends and colleagues who can help you. Then, thank them frequently and pay them back with loyalty and time as often as possible.

### Describe your office environment to us. Is it a normal, traditional-style office?

A normal office these days is more like a little town, and that's what we're striving for in our new—and too expensive—offices. We want lots of common space and informality that encourages people to "move in" and relax. Creativity flourishes when pressure subsides, allowing people to look out a window and say the dumbest thing that pops into their heads.

### Many business ventures are inspired by great leaders or other business start-up stories. Can you point to any inspirational models for your business?

*Ball Four* was pretty inspirational to me in the seventh grade, because it made me see that behind all great institutions there are real human beings, each with a full complement of weaknesses and stories to tell. And lots of curse words. This must be why I'm so into exposing the man behind the curtain of the media monolith.

### Where do you see the Internet going? And how will this vision affect your website?

Old Web is a jumble of information all crammed into one interface. It's a blur with no discernment, almost as if it's saying, "Look at all this stuff we can get our hands on now!"

New Web is simpler and cleaner. There's still a ton of choice, but not such a barrage of noise that viewers feel overwhelmed. And I do mean viewers, not users. The new Web is multimedia, with sound, pictures, animation, and text, all contributing to an immersion experience. Your computer—and eventually your set-top box and your handheld—should soothe you by giving you a sense of control over your world. Like a clean desk with all the stuff in the drawers, information should be easily accessible.

Old Web will get you all jangly, but I'm amazed at how my Blackberry wireless actually lowers my pulse rate when I'm riding in a cab on the way back from a business lunch. I don't have to fret anymore about all the emails that have piled up in the past 90 minutes. I can scroll down and confirm that, indeed, none of them were that crucial anyway.

I'm not a technologist, though I'm an avid employer of technology, and that's the proper perspective, I think. Old Web showed off the technology and put the viewer last. We're reversing that now.

# 17

# MeTV.com

*Power networking redefined*

ONE THING THAT AMERICAN enterprise has dominated world-wide over the years is entertainment. And MeTV is keeping the tradition of outstanding entertainment networks alive.

This site provides the starting point for a sampling of music, TV shows, sports clips, and all kinds of videos. You can link to shopping sites, read movie and TV trivia, and find out what's on television. But all that is just the front door to a technology company that is attempting to redesign the way the world takes in its entertainment. How?

With the help of MeTV, your telephone company can provide the same entertainment on demand as cable TV, plus much more—and not just on your PC.

Let's face it. All the hype about downloading the latest films to your PC is for the birds. Nobody kicks back in an office chair to watch a movie. Wait, though. What if you could download video to your computer and then send it to your TV? That's where your easy chair, couch, kids, and significant others are located.

Well, MeTV allows you do just that. Will the private network of your local phone company become the next pipeline for all kinds of entertainment?

MeTV thinks so and has blazed the trail in this techno-garden of opportunity. We spoke to Jeff Pescatello, who founded the company, to find out just what his vision is all about.

**First off, tell us about your firm and what we can find on your website.**

There are two sides to MeTV—a traditional dot-com and the private network division, which is the real focus of our company. The dot-com side acts primarily as a promotional vehicle for movie studios, record companies, and television networks to promote their fresh new content to our broadband audience. It also has a secondary purpose in that it showcases the public face of MeTV, demonstrating some of the technology and services that we offer.

The dot-com side is also strongly linked to our relationships with broadband ISPs (Internet service providers). We currently provide 17 DSL (digital subscriber line) providers with the latest trailers, music videos, and TV previews through a co-branded page that changes each week. It's a good situation for all of the parties involved. The content providers get their content delivered to a much wider audience together with real-time feedback. The broadband ISPs deliver to their customers the latest content available, thus helping them to justify both their services and the need for broadband access. And MeTV gets to build its customer base and its relationships with content providers and distribution networks.

The major focus of the company, however, is the secure private network division. MeTV's major goal is to create a sort of cable TV company within the private network of a telephone company. This way, the phone company can effectively compete for cable company subscribers by delivering on-demand programming through an IP (Internet Protocol) network to a customer's TV set, together with VCR-like functionality and a remote control-based interface.

We know that this is going to be a huge market for the future, and MeTV has positioned itself as a market leader in the area. Today we are focusing on the on-demand market because the infrastructure is there to support that type of business. The major challenge, though, is broadband penetration—it can never happen quickly enough! And the quality of the service itself. The various broadband providers deploy their networks at different bandwidths to suit their business models and biases. This ultimately restricts the rapid uptake of the MeTV service, but we do know that these problems are lessening with time.

### Can you tell us about yourself and how you came to found this business?

I began my foray into the entertainment industry after serving in the Airborne Ranger Division and completing various intensive military training programs overseas for two years. In 1985, I joined a radio station that my family had purchased. I started as a salesperson and worked my way up through the ranks, gaining experience and knowledge over several years.

Eventually, I started my own station by filing for an 80-90 FM radio license in 1988. The license process should have taken only two years, but it took twice as long due to government bureaucracy. I finally obtained the license in 1994 after a lot of very hard work. Over the next two years, I built the business from the ground up and made it into a market leader. I then sold the company for an excellent profit.

Although radio was a good business to be in, it certainly wasn't the industry for me to spend my life in. High technology was the future, so I worked for a telecommunications manufacturer for two years to gain the knowledge and skills I believed that I needed. It was then that I started to see the potential opportunities of the Internet. After a lot of research and discussion, I put together the MeTV idea and committed myself to the next stage in my business career.

*How exactly did your firm and its website come to be?*

At the beginning of 1998, I started jotting down notes on ideas that eventually gelled to become MeTV. I sent them to my brother-in-law, Martin French, who worked for Alcatel in Paris, and asked him for his thoughts and feedback. He understood it instantly and totally bought into the whole concept, adding his take onto it as well.

At this point we needed to get some of the ideas down on paper. I understood very well the value of a business plan, so I started drafting one in my spare time while traveling on business trips. Martin and I kept sending a revised plan back and forth. Finally, while attending a Real Networks conference in San Francisco at the end of May 1998, I realized that the time had come to turn the ideas into reality. It was not a matter of whether I could afford to do this. Rather, could I afford not to?

I called up Martin and told him it was time. When he asked how soon could I get to Paris to discuss it all, I said tomorrow—and I was in France 24 hours later. For the next two days solid, we fleshed out the idea.

Once we agreed that the time was right, we both quit our high-paying jobs the next day to start MeTV. One month later, Martin left France, I organized the office space and equipment, and we started MeTV. One week later, we hired our first employee.

*Where, when, and how did you first get the idea for your business?*

Well, as I told you, after selling my radio station, I worked for a telecommunications manufacturer. I was sent to Vancouver to oversee a high-profile cabling system that was being installed. The company there had asked that the system be capable of delivering video over simple twisted-pair cable, and I was heavily involved in making this happen.

Then, a few weeks later, I attended a conference where I saw high-quality streaming video for the first time. On the plane trip back, I made the connection and realized that there was a potential cutting-edge business opportunity here. I realized that if video could be delivered over twisted-pair wire on an intranet, it could certainly be achieved on the Internet.

Business ideas are often about making a connection between multiple experiences and industries. MeTV was definitely one of these.

### Who are your customers? Are they individuals? Businesses?

We have three types of customers—consumers, telcos (telecommunication companies), and content creators.

Our customer base certainly includes consumers for the dot-com and the network sides of the business. Primarily, these consumers are early adopters from professional backgrounds, who have either the foresight or the need for broadband Internet access. However, they are often disappointed with the lack of broadband-focused services to go with their high-speed access.

We can be classified as a VASP (video applications service provider) because we provide a turnkey solution for telephone companies and DSL resellers. These solutions get them into the video business at a very cost-effective price, as well as allowing them to increase their revenues by offering MeTV service. Our system is fully scalable, so as the telephone company grows its base, the MeTV system grows with it.

Content creators, such as movie and music studios, are important to us as well. We provide a suite of software and analytical reporting tools for them to obtain an accurate measurement of who is watching their content and where, and whether these end users actually like or dislike that content.

### As you reflect back on the growth of your company, what were some of the biggest obstacles you faced in getting off the ground?

Well, I believe there are three obstacles that face every start-up at some point in its development: the concept, personnel, and, of course, money.

The right concept for many start-ups is a difficult hurdle. You have to make sure that your ideas are solid, and you must keep your focus at all times. It's easy to become distracted by other opportunities that come your way as you progress. We have always remained true to our original concepts. Although we have made changes as we've learned and developed, they have always been in line with the goals of MeTV.

Secondly, personnel can be an obstacle to growing successfully. Finding the right staff at the right time is often difficult in the early stages. Luckily, we have never had this problem. It seems we have always chosen well, and there was a previously untapped skill pool in our Connecticut area.

Our biggest obstacle has been money. In today's market, VCs (venture capitalists) and investment banks should have their mottoes read "we take no risks," or "we invest only in already successful companies." Every day the criteria by which they judge a company for investment changes, and it has been a major learning curve to understand their requirements for investment.

Fortunately, I have been through the start-up process before. We have built the company with my own money (that's putting my money firmly where my mouth is!) together with angel money. Ultimately, this will pay off for us, and we will retain a bigger piece of the pie.

Now that we're up and running, I am starting to get calls from investment banks trying to get our business. We still have a long way to go and some tough decisions to make, and it certainly won't be easy. But for every day we execute our business plan, we become a stronger and more viable company.

The great thing about a start-up is the adrenaline rush you get from the risk and uncertainty. That keeps you going, plus the strong belief that any problem you may face can be overcome by flexibility, creative thinking, and the utmost faith in yourself and the people that you surround yourself with.

**What are some of the biggest successes you've experienced in taking your site to where it is?**

I think one of the critical programs we started was our DSL enhancement program. The program itself does not matter, so much as what it can accomplish for a client company. In our case, we first looked at what our customers needed. Then, we designed a program around those needs that was simple for us to sell and implement, plus easy for the DSL company to use as a selling tool to its customers. This was a very simple approach to getting customers, and it didn't take a lot of time or money to put in place.

Currently, we have more than 100,000 registered broadband users with a 384 kbps or faster connection, and we pick up about 1,500 new broadband users each week with very little promotion or advertising. We've taken this grassroots approach to our business, because we just didn't have millions to blow on advertising.

There have been many successes so far, some small and some bigger. In many ways though, every day that we're here, providing a service, employing our staff, and developing cutting-edge technologies is a victory. That's always rewarding.

**Is there anything you'd do differently if you had the chance to do it all over again?**

Hindsight is the most wonderful thing, and yes, there are things that we would have done differently. I think I could have saved some money knowing what I know today, but in our particular business there was no model to go with. There was no software we could buy off the shelf, so we really had to create everything from the ground up.

Now we're looked at as a market leader. So, I guess that money we spent learning the business—or really creating a new industry—was a small price to pay. We are in the envious position of being one of the first to market, which will ultimately help us with market share.

### What advice would you offer to someone wanting to start an Internet business?

This is the fourth business I have started, and none of them were easy. I cannot stress enough the importance of a business plan, because it helps to clarify what you're trying to accomplish. You, as the entrepreneur, will need to explain your venture to others to get them to buy into your idea, and the only effective way to do that is to know your business plan intimately. You will also need to adjust your business plan according to market conditions and your natural learning curve. However, the business concept should not change so drastically as to change your initial concept completely.

If you are planning to start your own business, make sure you have some experience in the business you are planning to start or enough capital behind you to learn the business. Also, make sure you have enough money to both bring your idea to fruition and fund the company for the first year. Whatever capital you think you need in your initial projection, it is probably not enough. Always overestimate.

Secondly, surround yourself with talented and motivated people. Don't take just anyone. If necessary, wait until you can get the right person as it will pay off in the long run. Your personnel are the very heart of your company, but run a tight ship. Hire employees only when you absolutely have to, even if it means working nights and weekends for the first year until you have cash flow.

Cash flow is king. If you're making money, you can do what you want with the business, and it is that much easier to expand the business. Obviously, expense management is essential. Every dollar counts, so don't waste them. Once they're gone, that's it. Set monthly budgets and stick to them even if that means getting creative when paying your bills. Most bigger companies will give you a break on paying a big bill by spreading out the payments, as long as you are making an effort to pay them.

Also, watch your lawyers. You definitely need them, but make sure you know what they're doing. Lawyers can go through money like Grant went through Richmond! And finally, never take no for an answer. Perseverance, stubbornness, and confidence are the three keys to success.

### What is your office environment like? Are you set up like a traditional office?

Some days you can come into the office and almost everyone is dressed up in suits and ties. That usually means there are bankers or business partners coming in. Normally, we all dress business casual, although we don't really have a strong dress code here. It's not unusual to see Hawaiian shirts and shorts in the summer.

It really is a team effort here, especially when we're trying to meet a particular deadline for a product launch and everybody's in and we're going for it. As a manager, you need that team spirit and dedication to the overall goals. I was very lucky from the start, as the initial hiring weeded out the people that didn't fit. When we hire someone, we want them to buy into the MeTV philosophy. Everyone that came to MeTV has made a personal sacrifice and totally bought into our idea and concept. Without that type of commitment, MeTV would not exist.

If you were a fly on the wall in our offices, you would see quiet studious moments as our technical team gets on with manufacturing the product, as well as moments of excitement as new developments become apparent. There's almost always a constant background hum of ongoing discussions directed at making our dream a reality.

**Often business ventures are inspired by great leaders, books, or other business start-up stories. What has inspired you?**

I would instantly say *The Art of War* by Sun Tzu. Read it before you start a business, because business is much like war. This book reinforced my understanding that there will be easy battles and tough battles. So, as a leader, you must surround yourself with quality managers that are capable of making critical decisions. At the same time, though, there must be a clearly defined chain of command, plus an open communication and information exchange between managers and employees.

You must also know when a battle cannot be won and be prepared to adjust your focus or plan of attack. This means that sometimes you may even become an ally with your enemy to get what you need or want. You must know your enemies, of course, both their weaknesses and their strengths. Also, it is never a good idea to attack a stronger opponent head on as it will only cost you valuable resources. What more can I say—read the book!

**As you look ahead, where do you see the Internet going? How will your website be affected?**

The common wisdom is that the Internet will be ubiquitous, interacting with every part of our lifestyle whether entertainment or work, and that it will be connected to every appliance we use.

In our industry, the Internet will be the preferred medium for broadcast entertainment, whether on-demand or scheduled programming. You'll be able to access that entertainment on your TV, computer, PDA, WAP (wireless application protocol) device, or even by using some of the cool things that IBM is working on for the future, such as wearable jewelry interfaces.

In five to ten years, I think on-demand will be the normal way of getting information and entertainment. It will be like email today—how did we live without it?

*Vitality shows not only
in the ability to persist,
but the ability to start over.*

*— F. Scott Fitzgerald*

# 18

## Mile High Comics

· · · · · · · · · · · · · · · · · · · · · · · · · · · · · · · · · ·

### *Comical all the way to the bank!*

THE BUSINESS OF COMIC BOOKS is comical all right. Listening to Chuck Rozanski, the president of Mile High Comics, Inc., will make you believe that work can really be play. And a hobby can be a business—big business.

Mile High Comics is one company that went from "brick and mortar" to "click and mortar" without demolishing the brick and mortar. The company still operates several comic book stores, but it did what any established business can do in the new Internet economy—expand.

The website doesn't have the feel of gourmet coffee and blue denim shirts embroidered with a dot-com coat of arms, but there is certainly a zeal for superheroes and colorful characters zooming about to save the day.

Venture capital for Mile High Comics amounted to what Chuck had on him in 1974—about $800 in cash and 20 boxes of old comics. But he discovered that comics are big business and a global business at that. In fact, Chuck Rozanski has done what many of us dream of. He's turned his hobby into a living.

**Please tell us about your company and what kinds of things can be found on your website.**

I founded Mile High Comics, Inc. in 1969 at the age of 14. Sales have grown from a few hundred dollars in 1969 to over $5 million in 2000. Our site is designed with collectors in mind, and our goal is to provide easy access to a completely searchable database of more than 250,000 comics, action figures, movie posters, and the like.

We currently stock about 90,000 items from our database and offer an automated "want list" program for the items not in stock. As those items are purchased and entered into our online inventory, interested collectors are notified by automated email.

To make it easy for collectors to find exactly the comic they're seeking, we've begun a program to scan the cover and the first three pages of every comic ever printed. We're presently at more than 100,000 scans, all done at 600 dpi (dots per inch) with more scans being added each week. We're also creating a bibliographic database for every comic ever printed. This will allow collectors to search by creator, character, date, and other criteria.

In addition, we operate the largest subscription service for new comics in America. Subscribers can visit our site to view upcoming products and add or delete subscriptions from their accounts. In the near future, they will also have real-time access to their subscription list and their account balances.

**How did the company and your website come to be? Is there an interesting story behind your start-up?**

Mile High Comics was originally founded to help me pay for additions to my own collection. By the age of 19, however, I decided to make comics retailing my lifelong career. I had four stores by the time I was 21, and when I turned 25 in 1981, I was the largest comics retailer in America.

Despite this early success, Mile High Comics was nearly bankrupt in the fall of 1996. We had become a traditional catalog-based mail order house, but those economics were no longer working. During 1996, we were losing cash in excess of $1,000 per day. At the end of 1996, we finally ran out of cash, and I had to go to our bank and plead for time.

I explained that I had a plan for converting Mile High Comics from mail order to online sales, which was a pretty radical concept at the time. My bank agreed to give me six months. To generate the cash for the transition, I was forced to lay off 40 percent of our staff, including some staff members who had been with us for more than ten years. That was very painful, but it gave us the positive cash flow we desperately needed to convert completely to online sales.

Within 15 months, we no longer printed any catalogs, but we had a higher level of sales. By eliminating the printing and mailing costs associated with catalog sales, we were able to return to a strong level of profitability, and the rest is history.

### Looking back, what were some of the biggest obstacles that faced your company?

Starting with absolutely no working capital was a real drag. I opened my first retail store in 1974 with $800 in cash and 20 boxes of old comics. Building up working capital from that point was very much like crawling through broken glass.

### What about your biggest successes?

That's easy—replacing our catalog gross sales with online sales in only 15 months.

### If you could do it all over again, what would you do differently to bring the business where it is today?

Originally, I heard about the Internet and online selling in 1995. A key member of my staff was against the idea, however, and continually threw obstacles in the way of getting our site up and going. She ultimately quit, soon after I forced her to register the site in the fall of 1996. I wish I had forced the issue earlier, as I think we could have made a lot of progress during early 1996. Maybe I wouldn't have had to fire all those people at the end of the year. I guess I simply relied too long on the opinion of someone who was very knowledgeable, but wrong.

*So many people in this world have a passion for a business of their own. What would you offer as advice to entrepreneurs, Internet-based or otherwise?*

Specialize. Definitely specialize and become absolutely the best in a selected niche. Then build out from there.

*Often business ventures are inspired by great leaders and other business start-up stories. What has inspired you?*

I read the life story of Meyer Rothschild when I was about 13 years old. He founded the entire Rothschild dynasty on the basis of providing rare coins to the Landgraf of Hesse during the 1700s. That was very inspirational.

*What do you make of the Internet? Is it mania?*

No, it is not mania. I believe there is a growing realization that the advent of online shopping, and online auctions in particular, is the greatest single change to the way goods and services are transacted since the advent of the suburban shopping mall during the late 1940s and early 1950s.

*Do you feel the Internet is truly changing the way business is conducted in our world, or is it overhyped?*

In my opinion, it is *under*hyped. As an active participant in online retailing, I am totally overwhelmed by the magnitude of the changes I see in the way that I can make my goods available to people around the world. Prior to our Internet sales, we were losing money as a traditional catalog retailer. By utilizing email and a very primitive website, we earned a small profit in 1997. During 1998, we worked very hard to improve our website and subsequently had the best year in the history of the company.

I believe 1999 will be far better. Internet sales for January should finish up over 300 percent from 1998. Bear in mind, too, that these profits were realized after all Internet setup expenses (over $200,000) were accounted for, including buying our own server.

*It's 20 years from now. Where will your company be, and where will the Internet be?*

I believe Mile High Comics will gradually dominate the world-wide market for many collectibles. I have a policy of reinvesting all profits earned right back into the company. At least part of those earnings will be invested to aggressively improve our fulfillment services. We are also cutting deals with other companies to mutually expand Internet traffic to our sites. If this continues for 20 years, I can't comprehend how large we could grow.

In regard to the long-term impact of the Internet, I think it may well spark economic wars between the United States and other nations. American entrepreneurs are embracing the Internet at a far faster and more aggressive pace than their contemporaries in other lands. As a result, we are dominating commerce in the huge market consisting of consumers from other countries. For example, between our website and auctions, Mile High Comics no longer needs to contemplate the horrific expense of setting up a brick-and-mortar store in Tokyo. We can now reach those customers for free!

It's also critical to understand that most of the international small package freight forwarders are American companies. Because of the way their rates are structured, we can ship to Tokyo far cheaper than a company from Tokyo can ship to Denver. For example,

American consumers will probably find only a few Japanese commercial websites or auctions, but Japanese consumers are already being overwhelmed by the range of American goods and services.

Sooner or later, this is going to have a dramatic impact on our balance of trade. That's when the political infighting over the future of the Internet will get very interesting. Can other countries put Pandora back in her box? I doubt it. The country that dominates the Internet will dominate the world. America is far ahead of the pack at this time.

***Do you believe that online auctions are impeded by the fact that many collectibles, such as furniture (a major part of the secondhand market), are not easily sold online?***

Not really. Even items like furniture can benefit from online exposure by driving regional traffic into brick-and-mortar stores, for example. Obviously, small items are better suited to auction selling.

However, having larger items listed should lead to a new business in large-item shipping. The problem is not the size, but rather the lack of current accommodation on the part of most shipping companies. This will change in response to growing demand. If you know that you can ship an item by having someone else take care of the packaging and freight, you're much more likely to engage in that business. Then there's the problem of cost. For our part, we don't plan to offer large items except in very special circumstances.

# 19

# Multicity.com

. . . . . . . . . . . . . . . . . . . . . . . . . . . . . . . . . . . . . . . . .

*Bringing businesses to the Web
in most any language*

ALAIN HANASH STARTED this company in his basement. Don't
you just love it! And if there's ever a tale of the pursuit of the
American Dream, this is it.

Alain claims he didn't fall into the "Internet hype trap." He continues to treat funding, the business, and its progress with utmost care. It's a big world out there, and Multicity.com seems to
know it. So much so, that it built a business around the big
world around us.

Alain has built a great business that has opened up the lines of
communication to so many. Listen to him tell the story of how
it all happened.

**Can you tell us about your firm and what we'll find when
we visit your site?**

Multicity.com specializes in developing multilingual Web technologies, including communications and e-commerce applications. Basically, website owners and businesses can come to our
website and obtain a tool that can be seamlessly incorporated
into their websites, but which is hosted and maintained by
Multicity through our ASP model. These tools include auctions,

chat rooms, message boards, instant messaging, Web polls, and profile matching.

In addition to providing hosted solutions, we also provide our tools in different languages. For example, our chat rooms are available in up to 17 languages, and they come with an instant translation capability, which allows users to communicate in real-time in different languages. In this way, a group of individuals can communicate in six different languages at the same time! The six available languages for instant translation are English, French, German, Spanish, Portuguese, and Italian.

Visitors to Multicity.com can take advantage of the opportunity to join existing multilingual discussion groups through our global network, or they can create a new discussion group through the use of our In-the-Box technology. This technology enables consumers to create and distribute Web-based tools such as chat rooms, Web polls, or auctions through their email without having to own or maintain a website.

***Tell us a little bit about your background and how you came to found this business.***

I was born in Rochester, Minnesota, to a Lebanese father and a French mother. My family traveled and lived in many different countries, including France, Lebanon, Saudi Arabia, and the United States. I attended American University where I obtained a B.S. in biology, and then I obtained a masters degree in engineering from Cornell University. Given my international background, I wanted to create a website that helped lower existing language barriers as well as facilitate cross-cultural communication. I wanted to create a site that allowed people to meet and communicate, regardless of their native language and country of residence. The reach of the Internet provided the perfect platform for developing such a "global village."

***How did your firm and its website come to be?***

As with many Internet start-ups, Multicity was started in the basement of a house. Prior to starting the company, I had worked as a consultant for Ernst and Young. I happened to be in a lonely hotel room in Manchester, England, when I decided to quit that job and move from New York City to Washington, D.C., and start working on my company. I spent nearly a year in the basement developing the technology and the idea behind Multicity. Today, the company's vision reflects its founders' multicultural background.

By the time we raised our first round of financing, we had a fully developed and deployed business plan with tens of thousands of users of our products. So, when we finally approached a VC, we secured our first million dollars in less than 10 minutes after presenting our plan to the managers of the Draper Atlantic venture capital fund.

*Where, when, and how did you first come up with the idea for your business?*

This idea was born in early 1997 while I was on an international project assignment for Ernst and Young in Manchester, England. Some of the concepts for this idea I had developed earlier during my work on Internet-based videoconferencing software at Cornell University. The premise of the idea was to attempt to leverage technology and the Internet to develop an easy way for people to communicate with one another regardless of their language or cultural differences.

*Can you tell us about some of your customers? Where are they from and what do they order?*

Because our products and services cater to both consumers and businesses, our customers come from a broad range, including entertainment, science, pharmaceutical, and job-recruiting websites. Consumers have the opportunity to join our site and meet and communicate with people from around the world.

They can join existing conversations or start their own discussion group by using our innovative In-the-Box technology.

Webmasters and businesses can also integrate our products on their own websites and offer all our services to their own consumers. These consumers will not only have access to multilingual technologies, but they will also have the opportunity, through the lateral connectivity of our network, to seamlessly communicate with users from other websites around the world.

A Webmaster can simply log into our website and customize a tool. Then, we'll deliver a few lines of code, which are pasted into the webmaster's site. Consequently, the tool will seamlessly appear on that webmaster's page.

**Looking back, what were some of the biggest obstacles your company faced in getting off the ground?**

Our biggest obstacle was the difficulty in finding and hiring first-tier employees. Given the competitive landscape of the Internet industry during the early stages of Multicity's development, it was extremely difficult to attract good employees. We wanted to make sure that we didn't hire simply for the sake of filling up office seats, which was a common practice among many start-ups. Those companies were attempting to ramp up their operations at light speed in order to catch the IPO window that was so widely open to many early Internet start-ups. This became one of the critical factors in the demise of many Internet companies.

**What have been some of the biggest victories you've experienced in taking the site to where it is?**

I think our biggest victories are:

- We were the first Internet company to introduce online multilingual communications products with instant translation capabilities.

- We were the first Internet company to have created a truly global network of users.

- Most importantly, we are one of the few companies that did not fall in to the Internet hype trap. We raised a large amount of capital and did not waste any of it on unnecessary expenditures. In a time of dot-com disappearing acts, this is an extremely relevant point.

**If you could do it all over again, do you think you would do anything differently?**

Well, I would like to have spent less time working and more time with my family and friends. Other than that, nothing!

**For someone wanting to start an Internet-based company, what could you offer as advice?**

The single piece of advice that I can give any entrepreneur is to be focused and extremely motivated. Motivation is the most critical success factor. It provides an entrepreneur with the persistence needed to develop an idea into a viable business. Consequently, motivated executives tend to be effective leaders.

The big advantage to starting an Internet business is the fact that, unlike traditional businesses, an idea can be implemented at a very low cost. You can be extremely innovative in the development and implementation of your idea by leveraging the low barriers to entry that the Internet offers.

**If I were a fly on the wall in your offices, what would I see? Do you have a normal office with a dress code and so forth?**

Actually, we have created a flat organization where ideas flow freely between all departments. Our business cards do not list the title of a particular individual because we believe that each employee should be given the freedom to think and work "out of the box." We have a casual dress code, and we spend a lot of time playing foosball or pool and organizing team luncheons. Such an environment is conducive to high levels of creativity, motivation, and productivity.

**Have there been any exceptional leaders, books, or other business ventures that have served as inspirational models for your business?**

The key elements needed to run an effective business are a clear strategy and aggressive execution, so an effective management team must have strong strategy skills. There are many interesting articles and books written by Michael Porter that can help executives understand and implement a sound strategic direction.

In addition, a good executive team must create a flexible organization that can rapidly adjust to internal and external factors, such as changes in the competitive landscape and new market conditions. I think Microsoft's Bill Gates is a great example of an effective leader who has established a strong, long-term strategy that has allowed him to dominate his competitors—for example, Windows and Excel vs. Lotus.

Gates has also created a company that can transform itself literally overnight when market conditions change. Think of Microsoft's entry into the Internet arena and how it regrouped the entire company's business units around an Internet market focus.

**Looking ahead, where do you think the Internet is going? And in light of this, where is your site going?**

The "true" revolution of the Internet will occur when it is being used as a medium for cross-border commerce, multilingual communication, and cross-cultural interaction. Then, I think the

Internet will move from a predominantly American medium to a truly global platform.

Lastly, I believe the desktop browser is going to lose ground to other access methods, such as wireless devices.

*In the middle of difficulty lies opportunity.*

*— Albert Einstein*

# 20

# Oingo.com

. . . . . . . . . . . . . . . . . . . . . . . . . . . . . . . . . . .

*Putting high-tech into searching*

GIL EBAZ IS A TRUE TECHIE. The website he's created looks like a search engine, but it actually exemplifies the technology that his company offers. In fact, his technical prowess has laid the foundation for a powerful technology that many other companies employ.

Not all search engines are created equal. Some employ different technology than others, but many of the top search engines employ Oingo technology, which is the core of its business. Oingo sells its search technology to domain registrars, portals, search engines, and content providers.

Have you ever wondered how you can plug a few words into a text box on a website and almost instantly receive a list of hits and other websites to visit? You owe it all to people like Gil Ebaz and his staff, who describe Oingo's website as "a highly detailed database of over 1,000,000 words and meanings linked by millions of relationships in a semantic network." Whew!

We talked to Gil Ebaz about how he happened to lay down the foundation for such a company.

**Can you tell us about your company and what a visitor will find on your website?**

Oingo Inc. is an infrastructure company that has created a new method of organizing, processing, and communicating information. Oingo has developed a broad set of intelligent applications such as meaning-based search, text classification, targeted advertisement selection technology, and domain name variation. These applications will revolutionize the way people and businesses interact with information.

At our website, www.oingo.com, you will find our ODP Search, which is a meaning-based search of the largest Web directory. That in itself demonstrates the value of our technology. Furthermore, you will find detailed information regarding our core technology, the Oingo ontology, which is a system of millions of words, concepts, and relationships that allows distinct elements of information (content) to be associated with one another by their level of semantic relatedness. In other words, this technology enables connections to be made between content elements that share a similarity in meaning.

This ontology is continually expanded and improved in one of two ways: (1) manually, with a dedicated team of 15 full-time linguists to ensure contemporary popular terms, such as sushi, VCR, and DVD, are added to our ontology every day and, (2) through our mechanical ontology expansion project, which enables new concepts and words to be automatically and organically added to the Oingo ontology. The site also gives in-depth information regarding all the products that have arisen from this core technology.

### Tell us something about your background. How did you come to start this business?

I cofounded Oingo with Adam Weissman in November 1998. Adam and I knew each other from Caltech. From our earliest days there, we loved to envision the future of technology and its impact on daily lives, economics, and society in general. I even remember a time when we discussed how the Internet could be easier to use if it had a graphical front end and how compelling it would then become. The birth of the Web prompted us to agree that the next time we had an idea for a technology that was:

(1) huge—it would change the world,
(2) challenging—something few people could do, and
(3) *cool*—it solved a problem that fascinated us both,

then we would drop everything and focus on it completely. That's what led to Oingo's meaning-based technology.

Prior to founding Oingo, I was the lead database architect at Silicon Graphics, where I managed a global effort to improve business processes at more than 100 sales offices worldwide. Before that I served as the principal information systems expert at a semiconductor manufacturer. Basically, I designed and developed scalable systems to run the in-house chip fabrication facility, which had potential revenues in excess of a billion dollars annually.

I also held positions at IBM and Sybase, where I actively defined company-wide standards for application development, database, and systems design. I graduated from Caltech with a double major in economics and engineering and applied science. While there, I won an award for outstanding research for thesis work done in the area of computer modeling in experimental economics.

### How did your firm and its site come to be? What stories can you tell about the actual start-up?

The company was started in a large house in the hills above Sunset Boulevard in Hollywood. We had rented the house because it had space for several of us to live in, as well as space we could use as an office. The casual atmosphere of the house was great until we outgrew it. By the time we left, almost every room had been wired with Cat-5 (Category 5 twisted-pair wiring), and Oingo workstations had taken over most of the house.

By then, those of us who lived there as well were quite happy to see the company "leave the nest." The inadequate air conditioning couldn't keep up with all the electronic equipment—summer days meant office temperatures reaching into the 90s! That's a feature we won't miss, but the pool was nice.

**Tell us about your customers. Are they individuals? Businesses? Where are they from and what do they order?**

Our customers are businesses. The applications stemming from our core technology are valuable to any business that hopes to achieve more efficient and intelligent translation of information and data. Thus, any company can be our customer.

To date, our strategy has been to focus on marketing and selling our products to the three customer segments that would derive the most immediate and obvious benefits. These segments include domain registrars, portals/search engines, and content providers. We have well over 40 customers and several hundred websites with light to medium traffic that have embedded our search on the open directory.

Our customers can currently order one of three main products:

- **DirectSearch**
  This product allows portals to better understand search queries and enables them to make a more intelligent response through dynamic connections to other content. The result is customized, personalized, and effective customer interactions.

- **DomainSense**
  With this product, domain name registrars can sell more real estate by intelligently recommending URL variations with similar meaning to prospective domain name buyers.

- **AdSense**

  Online businesses can maximize their search-based advertising revenues by using this product, which increases click-through rates by more effectively targeting customers based on their search queries.

**As you look back, what do you think were the biggest obstacles that faced your company in getting off the ground?**

The biggest obstacle was the paradox of the customer/credibility/capital triangle. It's very difficult to get started from point "A" when you have little money, no customers, and no track record. On top of that, we were marketing a new technology that had yet to catch fire.

**How about the successes you've experienced in taking the site to where it is?**

Our website saw a large boost in traffic when we won awards and received kudos in the press during 1999 and 2000. Recently, we were selected by *PC World* as one of the top five search engines in the world—and that's not even our primary business. In 1999, Oingo received the coveted *InternetWorld* Best of Show award for our DirectSearch product.

**If you were going to do it all over again, what might you do differently to bring the business to where it is today?**

I think we should have made sure the air conditioning in the house worked before we moved in. And, oh, yes, we also should have had it checked for termites.

Seriously, though, I think we have made the right decisions on the whole, and we are moving forward as we hoped. Truthfully, there's not much I can think of that we'd do differently.

*No business start-up is easy, yet many people have a passion for being their own boss. For someone wanting to start an Internet business, what advice would you offer?*

To start a business, it really helps to have investment capital. But what gives a business a great edge in attracting those dollars is just what you said—passion. How can you demonstrate passion?

Invest your own money in the idea; spend all your extra time on the business; quit your job and work on the idea; convince friends and family to invest small amounts of money. These are all risky propositions, but you just have to find the right balance between passion and conservatism.

*If I were a fly on the wall in your office, what would I see? Do you have a normal office? A dress code?*

What you'd see is a very dynamic office that was created by and for the employees. We recognize that the office is a place where many employees spend a large part of their day. Therefore, we've made every effort to design a space that is warm and collegial.

No, we certainly don't have mahogany desks and ergonomic chairs, but what we have is a creative use of space that supports a balance of productivity and a place to have some fun. For example, as a means to encourage and share creative expression, we have a "creative wall" where employees can display personal art. Several plant lovers are considering turning our office into a mini botanical arboretum.

Basically, our office space is a reflection of employee personality and culture, which can be best characterized as free-spirited, spontaneous, and imaginative.

*Many business ventures are inspired by great leaders and other business start-up stories. Who or what have you looked to for your inspiration?*

A hero in my eyes is anyone who was brave enough to stick to a revolutionary idea and spark a revolution that improved information exchange, business efficiency, and quality of life. Let's see, I could name Marc Andreessen, David Filo and Jerry Yang, or Larry Page and Sergei Brin (Google).

*If we look down the road a bit, where do you see the Internet going? How will your site be affected by the Internet of the future?*

People, and businesses even more so, spend huge amounts of time looking—looking for information, products, people, answers, and meaning. But only a very small amount of intelligence is built into the infrastructure of the Web itself.

To help businesses improve their services and to help people accomplish their goals, we have invented a technology that crystallizes any Web content down to its essential meaning. We know that this will have a profound impact on how the Internet is used, and it is exactly where the Internet is going.

The Internet will not only become more and more useful; soon, it will also become essential for a knowledge-based economy. I am looking forward to the time when the Internet is so helpful that it literally frees up time in our daily lives. Then we can use that extra time to focus on all the other important things that seem to get neglected.

*What we anticipate
seldom occurs. What we least
expect generally happens.*

*— Benjamin Disraeli*

# 21

# RightNow.com

. . . . . . . . . . . . . . . . . . . . . . . . . . . . . . . .

### *Putting the "service" in customer service*

GREG GIANFORTE KNOWS THAT customer service is critical to many businesses, but he also knows doing it right can be time-consuming and demanding. That's where RightNow Technologies comes in. Greg's company aims to provide a solution to the scores of inquiries that so many companies on the Web have to deal with daily. It seems he's really onto something big.

Greg is one Internet entrepreneur who knows what he's doing and does it well. "I am a software guy, and I've been in the software industry for a long time," explains Greg. "This is my fifth start-up." Wow! Now that's an entrepreneur. He has also taken advantage of the "located anywhere" aspect of an Internet business. RightNow Technologies is located in the big sky country of Bozeman, Montana.

Keeping the customers satisfied is a big business. When you have a product that can manage that task, you not only keep your customers happy, but management and employees as well. "I personally know that seven of our customers have received raises or have been promoted because they purchased our product," says Gianforte. "How great is that?"

Let's hear from Greg how it all came together.

*Tell us about your company and what we can find when we visit your site.*

In a nutshell, RightNow Technologies helps companies move customer service functions to the Internet.

Many companies find that they cannot keep up with email inquiries from customers or that they are losing business because prospects cannot find answers on their websites. These are the issues that we solve. For example, when Ben and Jerry's ice cream received 5,000 email requests that it could not answer, we installed our self-service information tool on the company's website. Now, over 90 percent of all the website's visitors can find an immediate answer without waiting for an email reply.

*Can you give us some information about your personal background and how you came to found this business?*

I'm a software guy and have been in the software industry for a long time. This is actually my fifth start-up. I love starting and growing companies. RightNow Technologies was started about three years ago, and we currently employ 340 people. We have been self-funded for most of our existence.

One thing I learned in earlier in life is that the Internet removes geography as a constraint to where you locate a business. After running companies in both the New York area and Silicon Valley, I decided to start one in a location where I wanted to raise my family. I had been coming to Montana for almost 20 years, so it seemed a logical choice. I currently live in Bozeman (Montana) with my wife and four children, ages 11, 9, 7, and 4.

*Now, what's the story behind how the firm and its site came to be?*

When planning the business, I started with what I knew. Because I knew software products, that was the first word in the business plan. But even three years ago, the only software opportunities were Internet software opportunities. So, actually, the first two parts of the business plan were "Internet software."

Obviously, that wasn't quite specific enough, so I started looking at areas of business that could benefit from automation. After some analysis and market research, I settled on customer service as the business function to automate. That then became the business plan—Internet software for customer service.

What I did next was to look at leading Internet sites and see what they were doing for customer service. I found little automation, and everything out there was home grown. So, I took the best ideas, built a prototype, and started showing it to people. Essentially, the prototype allowed customers to easily find answers on a given website, and it actually "learned" as more people interacted with the site. The result was that people could find their own answers and not have to send email or pick up the phone.

I kept calling people who I thought might be interested, and before I knew it I had 40 companies depending on my software. That's when I decided it was time to move out of my home and hire my first employee.

Up until that point, I had been wearing all the hats—programmer, salesperson, support, and management—with some help from my wife in keeping the books. I hired that first employee in March 1998. Today we have more than 300 employees and nearly 1,000 corporate clients, including Motorola, Lufthansa, Black and Decker, Nike, Sabre, Intel, and hundreds and hundreds of others in all industries.

**Can you tell us more about some of your customers? Where are they from and what do they order?**

Well, here are a few examples of our customers:

- The Social Security Administration gets about 68 million telephone calls per year, but the amount of email was overwhelming the staff. After adding our tool to its website, one part-time person now handles all the email inquiries.

- By installing our product, the Air Force Reserve was able to avoid hiring an extra 30 people to answer repetitive questions.

- Xerox cut its inbound telephone calls concerning its scanner products by 60 percent.

- Big Planet is saving $100,000 every three weeks in long-distance charges.

**Looking back, what do you recall as the biggest obstacles facing the company while getting off the ground?**

One obstacle was that no one knew who we were. To combat that, we offered our product with a 60-day money-back guarantee and charged much less than the product was worth just to get customers. Also, early on we had to do a lot of evangelizing because people didn't know what problem we were solving. All that changed over time.

**What are some of your biggest victories in taking the site to where it is today?**

I think our biggest victory is our customer base—we are very proud of our customers. However, early versions of our website were very rough, and it has gone through various revisions.

We now have a site that is a resource for people interested in improving customer service via the Internet. It's filled with customer case studies highlighting how they are improving their business, reducing costs, and improving customer satisfaction.

### If you could do it all over again, is there anything you would differently?

Sure. There are always lessons to be learned. In retrospect, though, our company grew from one employee at the end of 1997 to 12 at the end of 1998 and then up to 138 at the end of 1999. We finished up the year 2000 with about 370 people. I'm not sure we could have gone any faster and still be standing.

One thing I would definitely do differently is plan better for growth as it relates to our physical facilities. It seems we are constantly waiting for our next building to be completed. As a start-up you want to conserve cash, but at one point we had people working in an old condemned elementary school and in the back of a real estate office.

### Many of the people reading this book would love to have a business of their own. For those wanting to start an Internet company, what could you offer for advice?

My advice would include the following:

- Make sure you have a business proposition that has a clear customer benefit.

- Focus on sales—if you can't sell it to someone, you have nothing.

- Don't spend beyond your means.

- Maintain some balance in your life—this is a marathon, not a sprint.

- When you have a success, don't forget to celebrate.

### What about your office environment? If I were a fly on the wall in your offices, what would I find?

A fly on the wall would find a fast-paced environment where people are enjoying what they are doing. We set really high expectations and then work hard to exceed them. It sounds cliché, but we really put customers first and spend a fair amount of time figuring out how to exceed their expectations.

If you came to visit us on Friday, though, the programmers would be having a barbecue lunch by the trout ponds behind our campus headquarters.

**Are there any particular leaders, books, or other business ventures that have served as inspirational models for your business?**

My favorite business books are *Bottom Up Marketing* by Al Ries and Jack Trout and *The Art of War* by Sun Tzu. Then add some good old common sense. Necessity is the mother of invention, and the best strategies are born from difficult situations.

**What is your opinion on the future of the Internet, and how will your website be affected?**

The Internet has just begun. We're already seeing a preference among consumers to use the Internet as a way of communicating and exchanging information. I believe the Internet will quickly become the *primary* source for information on products and services across *all* industries.

I believe the Internet is more important to business than the railroad, the internal combustion engine, the assembly line, and most other prior inventions ever were. That being said, though, we're still in the cave dweller era of the Internet.

# 22

# seeUthere.com

*Event planning never had it so good*

JOHN CHANG'S COMPANY has redefined how the world of business organizes its meetings. His ideas have made it easy and efficient for companies of all kinds to "see you there"—whether at a trade show or corporate meeting—by using the horsepower of the Web to automate the process.

Though it may all sound like a Silicon Valley billboard, just read a few of his stories, and you'll see some real evidence of a new 21st century leader. John's the type of leader who allows risks, tolerates mistakes, and doesn't hang an erring employee on the front lawn of headquarters.

For example, an unfortunate employee in seeUthere's marketing department made a mistake that cost the company $70,000. When Chang was told about it, he asked, "Well, what has he learned?" and not, "How do we get him fired?" Wouldn't you just love to be working for a guy like that?

What's also interesting are Chang's roots. "My parents became entrepreneurs after fleeing the communists in China," says Chang. "They first emigrated to Taiwan, then to the United States. My father holds a Ph.D. in engineering, and he worked a long career in government. My mother, with help from my father, started a Chinese grocery store and two restaurants in Texas." If ever

America represented the land of milk and honey, it surely did for the Changs and their son, John.

Today, John continues to believe in the opportunities America offers, and he has built a great business that provides a great service. Listen to him tell his story, and you'll understand why seeUthere is on the move.

***Let's begin by talking about your firm and what we can find when we visit your website.***

As the leader in Web-powered event automation, seeUthere.com (www.seeUthere.com) targets professional meeting planners with a unique combination of services. On our website, we provide meeting professionals with three modules:

(1) Automation tools for managing event registration, confirmations and reminders, attendee surveying and profiling, and real-time status reports;

(2) An event marketing engine that lets planners create a branded event micro-site, manage one-on-one marketing campaigns, and expand their reach via email, fax, and mail;

(3) And the seeUthere Global Attendee Database™, which provides tools for evaluating ROI (return on investment) across multiple events, analyzing attendee profiles and attendance histories, and creating exportable reports that enable companies to integrate event data into existing CRM databases.

***Tell us a little about your background, and how you came to found this business.***

In my career, each job I've held has had some type of "Mr. Fix-it" or "Mr. Build-it" responsibilities. At HP (Hewlett-Packard), I had to fix a mediocre group and rejuvenate a mature, yet stagnant, business. At Acer, I was part of the team that established the retail PC business. Each job has followed the same pattern. Interwoven was the ultimate manifestation of this role. I was tasked with building a business that had virtually no product and no customers to a $13 million revenue run rate.

I never had the specific desire to start my own company or to be a CEO. However, the 1990s created a perfect environment for entrepreneurs—easy money, acceptance of failure, lots of surrounding infrastructure, and the like. As a result, I found myself gravitating toward start-ups, and eventually I cofounded a company.

My mentor is Dr. Leonard Liu, who was the highest ranking Asian at IBM after a 20-year career there. He became president of Acer Group (worldwide), then president and COO of Cadence, then chairman, president, and CEO of Walker Interactive. He is now the CEO of ASE and a member of the seeUthere.com board. Leonard encouraged me to start my own company, as did my father.

In addition to my role at seeUthere, I am a member of the board of directors for Afanti, and I am a member of the board of advisors for enFashion and OnePage. I am also a partner at an angel investment fund called StartingPoint Partners, which invests in early stage companies. The partners offer real entrepreneurial experience and commit to help each portfolio company—much more than typical VCs.

My wife and I have been married for more than ten years, and we have a son and a younger daughter. To balance the grueling work schedule of a start-up (and the frenzy of the Valley), I exercise regularly. I do push-ups, sit-ups, and run five times a week, averaging about 17 miles each week. I love skiing, and I try to ski with family and friends as much as possible in the winter. But, it's tough to maintain any sort of balance in a start-up.

***How did the firm and its site come to be? Is there an interesting story behind your start-up?***

The company was originally founded under the name TransComputing International by my friend and partner, Joseph Chen, on 31 July 1998. He recruited Hoselito Stankovic as VP of engineering soon thereafter, and I joined as Chief Operating Officer (COO) in August. Then, I convinced Ray Thackeray to join as VP of sales and marketing. Joe and Hosi started building the underlying foundation in late 1998 while I looked for funding. Meanwhile, Ray interviewed customers and gathered product requirements.

All of us shared a common vision for automating the grueling manual processes of event management, and, at the same time, we also hoped to build a new Internet platform on which additional applications could be deployed. This latter dream became a hindrance, however, so we scrapped the idea in early 1999.

We found that building a vertical application for event management was very different than building a generic Internet platform. The dichotomy became so intense in July 1999 that we scrapped all our code and started over, switching from Java servlets on Linux to Microsoft. The whole experience was a hard lesson on managing limited resources in an intense, fast-moving, highly competitive Internet environment.

Why did we believe in event automation? Well, Joe, Ray, and I had all served as volunteers for professional associations. We had also managed events in our previous jobs, and we hated the manual drudgery. So, we asked ourselves, "Wouldn't it be really cool to automate the whole process? Is there a way we can make it easy to send out invitations through all communications media and then allow invitees to RSVP anytime, anywhere, in any way?"

The Internet provides the ideal platform. It allows a company to deploy a "storefront" that is open 24 hours a day, 365 days a year, and it facilitates communications across all media. Without the Internet, a company would need to deploy a private network that generally costs ten times that of a public network, such as the Internet.

People always wonder why we started this business because we did not come out of the events business. Ironically, though, we did. We just weren't professionals at it. As I mentioned, we had all been volunteers, or we had organized events as part of our overall jobs. These experiences made us compassionate about the business. We understand how frustrating event management can be, and we wanted to make it simple for both the occasional event planner and the full-time professional event planner.

Three months after we launched our applications-based website in September 1999, MP3.com tried to acquire us. The acquisition process went on for three months before it unwound. During that time, Hoselito and his family went back to Australia, and Joe started another company. MP3.com later converted the acquisition into an $18 million investment because it could not use "pooling of interest" accounting.

Our business model has changed dramatically over the last few months. When we first started the company, we envisioned a free base service with transaction fees for value-added services. But this sort of business model takes three years to develop. The stock market crash in March and the subsequent market softness in Q4 2000 has made this "free plus value-added" transaction fee business model untenable. Instead, we have adopted a "subscription fee plus back-end transaction fees" business model. This structure is fundamentally the same as traditional enterprise software.

### Where, when, and how did you originally get the idea for your business?

We all helped various nonprofit and professional associations over the years, and the process of putting together an event was a huge pain! Just sending out the invitations was difficult. Licking thousands of envelopes and creating mailing labels took a lot of time.

Once we sent out the invitations, we had to answer innumerable calls all asking the same basic questions, such as the event location or the price of tickets. When we weren't getting enough people to attend, we had to buy costly direct mail lists at the last moment and then go through the whole process of licking envelopes and creating mailing labels again. Or, we pounded the phones to try to get people to attend. The whole process was really time-consuming and inefficient.

Because my partners and I came from technology backgrounds, we knew that we could eliminate a lot of the pain by using technology and the Internet as a platform.

**Can you tell us about some of your customers? Are they individuals? Businesses? What do they order?**

Most of seeUthere's customers are corporate and association meeting planners or independent event planners. They use our "professional" service for conferences, seminars, training courses, incentive events, and other professional meetings. Some of our clients include the AmeriCorps Alumns, the California Republican Party, Stanford University, Pier 39, MAXfunds.com, and Synergen.

We also offer a more basic invitation and RSVP management service for infrequent event planners and consumers. It is a self-service, pay-as-you-go transaction fee model that is called seeUthere Express™.

**Looking back, what were some of the biggest obstacles the faced your company in getting off the ground?**

In starting any company, you can't get funding without the right idea, the right business plan, or the right people. So, one of the biggest issues is to get people to buy into you so you can get funding. But the way that happens is to have the right idea, business plan, and people. It's sort of a catch-22.

Getting access to venture capitalists can be challenging, too. You either have contacts or you have to cold call, and I got very, very good at cold calling. I actually called one venture capitalist six to eight times a day, starting very early in the morning and calling late in the evening, hoping the secretary wouldn't pick up the phone so I could talk to him directly.

Another major issue is choosing the idea. I have a friend who listed 200 ideas and then prioritized those he liked. As seeUthere.com has developed, we have actually changed the idea several times. Part of the challenge is determining how to make money with your great idea and how to charge for your "better mousetrap."

### What are some of the biggest victories you've experienced in taking your site to where it is today?

Our biggest victory was being able to get such as amazing amount of funding when we did, because market conditions constantly change. We first got $3.7 million in funding in early 1999 with nothing but four founders and a great idea. Today, most companies are not funded at that level until you have a prototype. We were also able to attract great investors, such as Steve Jurvetson from Draper Fisher Jurvetson.

Our second biggest victory was actually launching the site. The team worked amazingly hard for a long time. In the final stretch before we "went live," all of us stayed continuously in the office. I had worked 66 continuous hours and along about hour 22, I wanted to sleep. But everybody else had already crashed on the futons and there were none available—so I went outside and jogged to stay awake. It worked, but four hours later I crashed! We had to put in such intense hours due to the build-test-build-test process that goes through multiple cycles. When it was all over, we were thrilled to tell the world that seeUthere.com was live—the first website focused on professional meeting planners.

Our third major victory was MP3's attempt to acquire us because that validated that we had built something valuable.

And lastly is the death of Evite, which had to sell its business because it didn't have a business model. This was gratifying to us, because everyone criticized us at our launch for being too professionally focused. These critics felt that our look and feel was too boring and business looking, and that we had too many features that were hard to use. At that time, Evite epitomized everything we were not. Now it's gone, and we're still going strong.

***If you had the chance to do it all over again, are there things you would do differently?***

Definitely. There are lots of things that I would do differently. First, I would like to have been more selective about my choice of cofounders and better able to understood their goals, exit strategies, and what they wanted out of a start-up.

Second, I would have been much more careful in selecting a platform. Instead of using freeware—Java servlets on top of Linux—I would have chosen a more stable platform.

Third, I would not have fallen prey to the new business model that people thought would develop on the Internet. I would have immediately gone to an ASP-hosted model and sold subscriptions rather than trying the experimental Internet business model, which was set up as a free service with value-added transactions. We only started selling subscriptions to our service in September of this year.

***Many people in this world long to run a business of their own. What would you offer them for advice?***

First, it is very important to recognize that the Internet is a deployment platform. It's a way to reach people, but it should not be thought of as a business. That distinction is what's behind the current dot-com fallout. People thought the Internet represented a new business, so they invested heavily and started all these crazy businesses that couldn't really make money.

At the end of the day, though, you need to stick to the fundamentals. The goal of a company like Hewlett-Packard, for instance, is to make a profit. Without a profit, you can't take care of your employees, your customers, or your investors—you can't do anything else, period.

You also need to ask what the compelling value of your business is to customers. How much will they pay, and can your business make a profit from that? Our company uses the Internet to deliver our services, but fundamentally we are an automation tool and automation service. Instead of handing over a software CD, we use the Internet to deliver the service.

Second, the service you offer had better be compelling. Find a customer problem that is so painful that they need you to solve it. If your service is a "nice to have," you won't be able to charge enough money to make a profit.

The analogy I always offer is chemotherapy. Why do people undergo this harsh treatment? Patients lose their hair, their white blood cells die, and they get nauseous. But the alternative is death. Cancer victims accept this treatment and endure the side effects because it keeps them alive.

Your service must do the same thing. To be profitable, it had better solve a great deal of pain. Don't focus so much on perfection. Focus on solving the problem and easing the pain.

**What's the atmosphere like in your offices? Do you have a normal office with a dress code and a water cooler?**

We have a lively and dynamic environment at seeUthere. There is certainly an hierarchy, but it's not an in-your-face structure. We try to keep the organization and the way we work as flat or egalitarian as possible. We also strive to conduct our business in a respectful, professional manner, but not to the point of being overly formal.

Employees are encouraged to take risks. We want then to be able to push back and say, "I don't think this is a good idea." I use Babe Ruth as an example. Most people know that he held the record for hitting the most home runs, but they don't know that he also had the most strikeouts.

Our executives manifest this culture by making fun of each other, by not pulling punches, and by being open—but never with disrespect. We have good camaraderie and cross-functional teamwork—engineering likes to talk to sales. People like one another and want to talk. We stay focused on the right things, such as winning and developing a profit. When people are focused on other things, politics and backstabbing can develop.

Everyone dresses casually, and we try to liven up the atmosphere by holding an all-hands meeting each Friday. It's an opportunity for everyone to hear about progress in the company. During this meeting, we usually recognize star contributors with the "scooter" award, which means he or she gets to ride the electric scooter around the office for a day.

We also try to counterbalance the grueling demands of a start-up with flexible hours and free dinner. Each evening, we bring catered food into the office around 7:30. It's a great opportunity for late-night workers to talk to others.

*Often business ventures are inspired by great leaders and other business start-up stories. Are there any great leaders, books, or other business ventures that have served as inspirational models to your business?*

I would point to the story of Bill Hewlett and Dave Packard. It's an amazing record with great anecdotes. At business school and at HP, we studied their style and the culture that they developed. The best description of a company's culture is in its anecdotes.

*Built to Last* by Jim Collin is a book about the best enduring companies (in terms of the best places to work and their longevity), such as Proctor and Gamble, HP, and Johnson & Johnson. The book talks about risk taking and building mutual respect.

I learned the importance of risk taking and customer focus at HP, and I have tried to apply it at both Interwoven (my last company) and seeUthere. At Interwoven, an employee trying to help a customer accidentally blew up the customer's last 48 hours of work. Obviously, that was not a good thing. The employee was talking about resigning, asking how do we apologize, and suggesting that we use him as a scapegoat.

My first question was, "What have you learned, and how do we fix the process so it never happens again?" In my view, we had just paid for a $10 million lesson, so we had to learn from that.

A similar incident occurred at seeUthere. Someone in the marketing department made a mistake that cost the company $70,000. When that story was relayed to me, I asked what had he learned, not how do we get him fired. I knew that the employee had the best of intentions and that he was working overtime. He had taken a risk and delivered awesome results, but he made one mistake. You have to focus on the good and the lessons learned, not on the mistakes. Obviously, you can't afford to repeat the mistakes!

**Looking ahead, where do you see the Internet going? And, in light of this, where do you see your website going?**

People are quickly starting to realize that the Internet is not a business, but a delivery mechanism, a platform for deployment.

Brick-and-mortar companies are realizing that it is another channel for distribution, and they are going to take advantage of that.

The Internet will continue to be a wonderful communications method, but it will also blossom as a computing platform. Application services will be available from any device at any time. You will no longer load software. Instead, you'll run applications over the Internet.

A great manifestation of this trend is seeUthere.com, which uses the Internet as a delivery mechanism. Ours is an application that could not exist before the Internet. You can run our application from all over the world and from all sorts of devices, but, fundamentally, the application is running on the Internet infrastructure.

As for our company, seeUthere.com will continue in the same direction, delivering services on the Internet and making them accessible to multiple devices that have access to the Internet. I predict that we'll see more ASPs like seeUthere in the future.

# 23

# Tyler-Adam.com

## The electronic cyber stop for all that glitters

BENJAMIN MARK and his company, Tyler-Adam, are proof that you don't have to be Silicon Valley cool to build a Web presence. Tyler-Adam sells jewelry, and Mark was able to go from brick-and-mortar to click-and-mortar without giving up the brick-and-mortar core of his operation. It's yet another example of the worldwide connectivity that a Web presence brings.

Mark is the quintessential entrepreneur who took what he already knew and used technology to enhance it. He bloomed right where he was planted, without taking on the undue risk that capital investment in new technology and the Web can bring.

Tyler-Adam's website is simple, but it works. There aren't any flapping icons or complicated gizmos—just a straight-talking jeweler with a dash of mom-and-pop merchant. Basically, the website supplements in-store sales with orders that might not have been received otherwise.

Mark has further enhanced the business with an e-zine newsletter designed to inform and attract both current and potential customers, but most of all, he's having fun with the Web. He likes to chat with his customers, even have dinner with them, and he enjoys learning about new technologies and how they can work for his company.

What's refreshing about Mark's story is that you don't get the feeling that he's out to conquer the world with his website. He has taken his time to both learn and then apply what he's learned, all the while holding on to his core business. With the help of the Internet, he's simply making his day job a better job.

We talked to Benjamin Mark to learn what he did and what he's currently up to.

**Can you give us a description of your firm and what we can expect to find on your site?**

This is primarily a jewelry site, so, of course, visitors find jewelry. However, I write a weekly e-zine entitled *Tidbits*, which many visitors go to. With regard to jewelry, there is a diamond search engine that enables folks to find a specific stone out of our stock. We also carry watches, antique-style rings, cufflinks, pendants, religious items, and so forth. I try to cover a pretty broad spectrum of jewelry.

**Tell us about yourself and how it is you came to found this business.**

When I was young, I was a ham radio operator. Then I got married, stuck my radio equipment in the basement, and forgot all about it—life, children, and all that. About four or five years ago, though, the Internet began to make itself known. I saw that it was the new frontier of tomorrow, so I jumped on it. I read HTML books, imaging books, photography books, and all that stuff—I really threw myself into it. Pretty soon, I put up a website, doing all the programming and the graphics myself.

To this day, my wife tells me it's the ham radio of my adulthood. I think she may be right. Anyway, it's easier to write an email than it is to send info via Morse code. I don't know how much I'd enjoy di-di-dah-ing at this point. I surf the Internet with ease, and I love it.

### Where, when, and how did you first get the idea for this business?

I started off in life as a diamond setter. Soon, however, I found myself doing a variety of services for my customers, until I eventually became a full-service contractor for jewelry manufacturers. In other words, I was manufacturing jewelry for jewelry manufacturers, using their materials and selling my labor.

After a while, I branched out a bit and began doing my own manufacturing. Then the Internet came along, and I set up the site. Today, I manufacture very little for the trade because I am concentrating those efforts on B2C (business to consumer) sales.

### Tell us about some of your customers. Where are they from, and what do they buy? Are they individuals? Businesses?

My customers come from all over—the U.S., Japan, Belgium, Romania, everywhere. Unfortunately, the opportunities for fraud abound, and I've gotten burned a few times. So, I'm selling less and less outside of the continental U.S. these days.

My most interesting sale (sounds a bit like *Reader's Digest*, doesn't it?) was to a customer who had read a weekly *Tidbits* article I wrote covering the topic of emeralds and their magical qualities. I had written the article tongue-in-cheek, of course.

Nonetheless, a gentleman in North Carolina emailed me asking if I could supply him with an emerald in light of its magical qualities. So, I sold him one for around $20—not a big sale. A week or so later, the same gentleman asked me for a sapphire. I took care of it, again for $20. Then another request, this time for a ruby, and I took care of it that, too.

There was silence for a few weeks, but soon another email arrived. He had seen a diamond on my search engine and was interested. To make a long story short, I sold him a diamond—over one carat—and then sold two more diamonds to friends of his. Later, we actually had dinner together when my wife and I drove down to Florida. I have met other folks the same way.

**As you look back, what were some of the biggest challenges facing you in getting your website off the ground?**

For me, it was learning HTML programming, Photoshop software, and photography. There are folks out there who are generous with information, but there are also those who want to maintain a mystical quality about their fields in the hopes of preventing competition. I met both kinds.

For the most part, though, I learned on my own. It wasn't difficult, but it was time-consuming. There were no automatic editing programs then, so you had to know your stuff. I didn't want to pay others to do the work for me because the cost would have become prohibitive.

**What about the biggest victories you've experienced while taking the site to where it is?**

Every time the phone rings or an email comes in, I do a silent victory whoop. It tickles me no end. When five or six orders come in at a time, I'm beside myself. It knocks me out!

**If you could do it over again, is there anything you would do differently to bring the business to where it is today?**

Considering the knowledge that was easily available then, the answer is no. If I were starting out with what's available now, however, I would probably use different vehicles to bring my site into being. Software is much more sophisticated today.

Of course, everything is dictated by finances. If I had unlimited funding, I would set up my own server. It's the right way to go if you have the bucks, because there are no restrictions behind it.

**No business start-up is easy, but for someone wanting to start an Internet business, what can you offer for advice?**

Read, read, read, and then read some more. The more you know, the less dependent you are on those that charge for their knowledge. Knowledge is free, and it's the most valuable weapon in anyone's arsenal.

**If I were a fly on the wall in your office, what would I see?**

Well, I used to run a 40-man shop when I first started playing with the Internet, but I subsequently moved into an office where I work alone. A fly would see a computer, a desk, some chairs, filing cabinets, diamond scales (modern and antique), a gold scale, a TRTL safe, and a mini-shop where I still work with my hands.

And you'd also see this guy, with a pleasant enough face and nice smile, sitting behind his desk, checking his email, and letting out a whoop every time something good comes in.

**Business ventures are frequently inspired by great leaders or other business start-up stories. Are there any great leaders, books, or other businesses that have inspired you?**

I wish I could say Dale Carnegie or something like that. Alas, I can't. I'm more of a fringe herd member. I plot my own courses and hope for the best. Sometimes it's good, sometimes it ain't.

**Looking down the road, where do you see the Internet going? And how will your website be affected?**

I can say without the slightest shred of doubt that the Internet is the world of tomorrow. It's going to change the face of this planet in every way—from e-commerce to information gathering and dissemination to communications and to who knows what else. The limits are unbounded.

We're going to have face-to-face live communications with our clients one day soon, and we'll be able to show and send holograms of our wares. I wouldn't mind living another 100 years or so just to see it all. I believe we live in the most astounding of times.

Hopefully, as I huff and puff, I can keep up with the technical aspects of this medium. I'm learning, though slowly, a program called Dreamweaver. It's today's industry standard for creating websites. When I have that mastered, I may revamp my site, or maybe not. I don't know.

As I go along, I see more and more of what customers want. My ultimate goal would be to set up a multi-ware site, much like a department store, where one-stop shopping prevails.

# 24

# WantedTechnologies

*The job search engine of job search engines*

IT'S AN INTERESTING CONCEPT—a dot-com that thrives when there are lots of layoffs and people are looking for jobs. David Tanguay, one of this company's founders, summarized it best when he said, "The hard times on the Net translate into good times for Wanted Technologies."

Take a moment to visit this site, try out the job search, and you'll discover that it's the granddaddy of job search engines. WantedTechnologies offers a great tool, and the company has positioned itself in an interesting way.

We spoke to David to learn more about his start-up.

**First of all, tell us about your firm and what we can find on your website.**

Wanted Technologies syndicates comprehensive and customizable solutions for e-businesses so they can power their own online career centers. We are able to do this because we developed the next-generation search technology for online vertical markets.

Our company licenses this technology to high-traffic websites so they can increase and monetize user retention. It has been very successful when applied to the online job-search market.

Today, we are based in Quebec City (Canada). The company was originally founded in 1997 by a group of high-tech entrepreneurs with backgrounds in computer science, business development, marketing, and finance. Wanted Technologies has since grown to more than 40 employees, with public relations offices in Los Angeles and business development offices in London. From the outset, our company has garnered international acclaim in the United States, Western Europe, Asia, and Oceania.

Wanted Jobs.com (our website) enables users to simultaneously query 280 online job sites in less than five seconds. Wanted Jobs provides access to more than 3 million job offers in North America, and in terms of added-value services, there is a job cart, a job agent, and advanced search options, i.e. a keyword search and a location search.

***Tell us something about your background and how you came to work in this business.***

Ian Delisle and I are childhood friends. We both studied at Université Laval in Quebec City, and we both received our bachelors degree in 1996. We also found ourselves working at the same company, SIT, as it was going belly-up.

At that point, we decided to turn to the Web to find new jobs. What a mistake that was! There were way too many sites, and you needed to log onto each site regularly to find new postings. We became so frustrated that we decided to create a tool to help job seekers find job opportunities more efficiently.

Once the tool was created, I took a leave of absence and tried to stir up interest in our meta-search tool. After a while, Ian quit his day job, and we launched Wanted Jobs in May 1998. I became CEO of Wanted Technologies at the age of 26.

***How did the firm and its site come to be? Is there an interesting story behind your start-up?***

As I mentioned earlier, Ian Delisle and I are the cofounders of the company, and it all started when we turned to the Web to find new job opportunities. That process was far from hassle free. We both hoped against hope to find a tool that would facilitate the job search via the Internet, but such a tool didn't exist. Therefore, Ian decided to create it, and his meta-search engine was the first one specifically tailored to the job market.

Once the tool was created, I became convinced of its marketability. So, I quit my job and started working (in a kitchen) on a business plan to present to investors. Ian kept his day job, but in his spare time he continued to develop the technology. After about six months, we both started working full time on the project, and six months later we hired our first employees. In May 1998, we launched Wanted Jobs Online, and the rest, as they say, is history.

**Can you tell us about some of your customers? Are they individuals? Businesses? Where are they from and what do they order?**

We syndicate comprehensive and customizable solutions for e-businesses to power their online career centers. Our clients are high-traffic portals and virtual communities that are willing to offer added-value services to their end users in order to increase stickiness.

For example, Hoover's (Nasdaq: HOOV), Sina (Nasdaq: SINA), Yep, Employment 911, Medster, ScienceWise, Recruiter Connection, Simple, and BizProlink all have career centers that are powered by our meta-search solution. Our client base is mostly in the U.S. with a few notable exceptions in Europe and Asia.

Most of the time, our clients want a meta-search solution specifically tailored to vertical markets. For example, Hoover's is a financial portal; Medster is a medical portal; and BizProLink has 124 virtual communities.

**What were some of the biggest obstacles facing the company in getting off the ground?**

I think the biggest obstacle was finding the courage to leave everything behind and start a new project from scratch. When you start your own business, there are no security nets. You need to accept the risk you are undertaking.

Once the decision is made to start a company, the first issue is to secure financing so you can promote your idea and try to get noticed. For two years straight, I worked 90 hours a week. The company was my whole life, and eventually all that hard work paid off.

Another problem we faced was that we did not come from a business background. Therefore, we gained knowledge of the B2B (business-to-business) markets by trial and error. The biggest problem of all, though, came as a result of the dot-com flameout. Our clients, partners, and investors wanted guarantees that we would not fold.

Because the growth of our company has been steady, however, our investors now think of us as a blue-chip investment offering long-term potential, high security, and moderate returns. Wanted Technologies is here to stay, and we are fast becoming a major player in the industry.

**What are some of the biggest victories you've experienced in taking the site to where it is today?**

There are a few victories we're proud of, but the biggest victory was obtaining the financing required to properly launch the company. In February 2000, we received a $3 million investment from various partners. Other victories include:

- In October 1999, we dethroned Monster.com as the driver of the online searches for Hoover's.

- In May 2000, Yahoo Internet Life! named Hoover's (which we power) as the best meta-search solution. We're really proud of that achievement.

- In August 2000, we signed Sina.com, the biggest Web portal in Asia.

- In October 2000, we moved in to the high-tech park in Quebec City. In the past year, our staff has more then doubled, as have our market shares.

*If you had the opportunity to start over, is there anything you would have done differently to bring the business to where it is today?*

Hmm, good question. It's not something you ask yourself every day, but, no, I wouldn't change a thing. It was tough getting the company to where it is, but it was also a great opportunity to learn and grow. Our steady growth is a sign that we were doing something right. Today, I don't regret a single thing.

*Many people in this world have a passion for a business of their own. What advice would you offer to someone wanting to start an Internet company?*

The most important thing is to write a business plan and to set goals for yourself. You need deadlines to make sure that you go where you need to go. You need to be able to pitch your idea succinctly, and you can't afford to count the hours you invest to promote your idea. Most of all, you business needs to be a labor of love.

*Tell us about your office environment. Do you have a traditional office with a dress code and water cooler?*

Our offices are painted in bright colors—hues of dark blue, orange, and deep yellow. The doors are always open, and the office furniture is stylish and made of wood. In general, the atmosphere is warm and pleasing to the eye. There's no dress code and employees have a flexible work schedule. Also, each employee owns shares in the company.

We exemplify the California model of organization, but we also follow certain basic notions of the Japanese model of organization. Everything is designed for maximum dynamism and innovation with an eye to stimulate creativity among the staff.

**Business ventures are often inspired by great leaders or other business start-up stories. Can you point to any leaders, books, or other business ventures that particularly inspired you?**

Like all other computer geeks, Steve Jobs was a role model for us. He always remained true to his convictions, and he stood by his ideas in both success and failure. What he did with Apple computers was quite impressive. The evolution of Apple computers is such an inspirational story—you know, the fabled David who through hard work became the fabled Goliath.

**Looking into the future, where do you see the Internet going? And in light of this, where is your site going?**

As you're aware, there's been a dot-com flameout, and e-businesses are going bust every day. Things are looking rather bleak for the Internet, at least in the short term.

The current situation is actually a great opportunity for Wanted Technologies, though. Websites are willing to try anything to induce stickiness, so our meta-search solutions have become increasingly interesting to many portals. For the present, at least, it seems hard times on the Net are translating into good times for Wanted Technologies.

# 25

# Winebid.com

*Buying fine wine online*

IT USED TO BE THAT A WINE connoisseur had to go through a lot of trouble to buy fine wines at a conventional auction. These customers had few choices. They could physically attend the auction, wait on a telephone, or send in a blind bid with only minimal background information about the vintage. Well, no more.

Luckily, the principals of Vintage Resource International recognized the problem, saw the opportunity for a business, and proposed a solution—Winebid.com, an Internet firm specializing in the auction of fine wines. Winebid aims "to provide an innovative method for wine enthusiasts to obtain aged premium wines in the most convenient possible way via your computer."

So, what is sold? A quick visit to the company website revealed a 1969 Domaine de la Romanee-Conti Horizontal Collection of Pinot Noir(A), 750 ml bottle, estimated auction price between $2,500 and $2,900. Also up for sale was a 1949 vintage Chateau Latour, 1er Cru Classe, 750 ml bottle, estimated price between $600 and $660. Do these prices sound low?

Well, don't judge too quickly. Winebid recently sold a case of 1982 Petrus for $13,500, and a case lot of twelve vintages of Screaming Eagle (three bottles from each of four consecutive vintages) sold for over $17,000.

Winebid is a wonderful site for wine aficionados, and even not-so-aficionados. The company has done a great job of making fine wines available to the world. We had the opportunity to speak to the company's principals and got their story about selling fine wine online.

**Can you tell us a little about Winebid and what you offer to someone who decides to stop at your website?**

Very simply, Winebid.com offers access. Prior to the Internet, access to this market was available only to the cognoscenti of the wine-collecting world. If you wanted to bid on the finest, most coveted wines in the world, you were forced to participate in the few wine auctions that existed at the time. Furthermore, one had to be in London, New York, Chicago, or Los Angeles to take part in these auctions.

Winebid.com is an Internet site where a 24-hour market has been created for wines. Now, no matter where you're located in the world, you can bid on the same wines that were previously available only in the above venues. As a result, Winebid.com has opened up the fine wine auction market to a larger, broader audience. Our website is also great for the person who wants to *sell* a collection of wine.

Another noteworthy feature of the Winebid site is that buyers have the flexibility to bid on and purchase wines in smaller quantities than a full case. Traditional, live auction houses require a buyer to purchase full-case quantities only.

**How did Winebid.com come to be? Any tales of start-up you'd like to share with us?**

Of course. Winebid.com began as the personal project of Charles Parsons. As a longtime wine collector who frequented auctions in Chicago and elsewhere, Charles decided it was time to sell off part of his collection. It was his son-in-law, Darren Nakos, who suggested simply auctioning them on the Internet. Charles thought, why not?

Darren, who was working full time in high-tech sales, created some basic auction software, and then registered and built the site. In September 1996, the very first auction took place. It consisted of 30 lots of Charles' wines, most of which were valuable California wines, but only a meager $5,000 or so was raised. In fact, nearly all of the wines were purchased by one gentleman.

Subsequently, the wines were packaged up and shipped out from a garage in Illinois, and . . . Winebid.com was born. It quickly became apparent to Darren and Charles that much more fine wine could be auctioned in this manner. At the time, no one else was selling wine on the Internet. E-bay and so forth were not yet household names.

The next few auctions consisted of only Charles' wines, but, eventually, other collectors contacted Winebid.com wanting to sell their wines. By the end of 1996, Winebid.com was expanding quickly.

*What are your customers like? Are they from all sorts of geographic and ethnic backgrounds?*

Winebid.com customers are wine lovers first and foremost. They belong to that relatively small group that has a profound interest in wines, loves to drink them, and has the disposable income to buy the best. Yet, Winebid.com's customers are somewhat different from the traditional wine auction house customer. They're slightly younger, and many have never stepped into a traditional wine auction house. Because of the uniqueness of the auction software utilized by Winebid.com, though, our customers don't need thousands of dollars to begin collecting.

The majority of Winebid.com customers come from the United States. Some ten percent are located outside the U.S., with the majority of that contingent located in the Far East. Winebid.com customers appear to have a higher than average household income.

We have never kept records or surveyed our clientele on their ethnic background. However, the gender profile of our clientele, just like the traditional wine auction market, is heavily skewed toward males.

*There's a perception that wine collecting is for the sophisticated dilettante. But for someone with an interest in fine wine, can your website help educate them as well as offer fine wine at auction?*

For the person interested in collecting or purchasing wines, it has always been very difficult to watch the fine wine market. There are only a few places to go to find out which wines are going up or down in value, what segments of the market are hot or cold, and other specialized information, and these places are not always up-to-date.

In contrast, Winebid.com has monthly auctions, and the results are posted immediately. Winning bids received at Winebid.com are very similar to those received at traditional auction houses, but they don't hold auctions as often as we do. As a result, a person interested in fine wine now has a place to go to get an idea of what the market is doing.

We also offer the fine wine lover in-depth information on collectible wines via our monthly *Winebid Report*. Currently, our company is focusing on the education and information element of our website, and we plan to expand that aspect over the next 12 months. Our goal is to become the website where you *must* go to get the best information on the finest wines in the world.

The Internet is the great equalizer when it comes to accessing products and information. Wine sellers could always get their products to an auction with little trouble if they truly wanted to, but they have a larger audience now. Internet auctions allow anyone, anywhere to get their hands on a bottle of 1947 Cheval Blanc. That was not always the case.

Online auctions, like the rest of e-commerce, are impeded only by the limitations of technology. There's no reason why furniture or other collectibles can't be sold on the Internet. The real issue for Internet auctions isn't technology, though. The issue is acceptance, and that is being overcome rapidly. A benchmark will occur when the major auction houses, such as Christie's and Sotheby's, enter the Internet world.

Success in the traditional wine auction arena is measured by the percentage of available wines sold at a given auction. Winebid.com has sold over 90 percent of all lots at its monthly auctions. That's an incredible achievement. Furthermore, Winebid.com has gotten the same prices for the exact same wines as those sold at live auction houses. In addition, we have broken numerous records for the highest price received for a particular wine.

*No business start-up is easy, yet many people in this world have a passion for a business of their own. For someone wanting to start an Internet business, what could you offer as advice?*

Perfect your customer service. The Internet always allows customers to go elsewhere with only the click of a mouse. Great customer service is the key to keeping them coming back to your website. Innovate or die! Someone is always ready to come along and do it better. If you don't innovate, someone else will—and your customers will notice.

*Failures are divided into two classes
—those who thought and never did,
and those who did and never thought.*

*— John Charles Salk*

# Marketing Tips

· · · · · · · · · · · · · · · · · · · · · · · · · · · · · · · ·

*Tips—we've got tips!*

IN THIS SECTION, I've included 15 meaty tips on marketing and small business strategies, plus 35 more tips on building your business. And for those who never get enough good information on growing a Web-based business, check out the 25 tips I've put together for building your website.

You see, getting any business up and going means that you can never stop learning. You have to learn before, during, and after you launch your business venture, and one of the most valuable exercises you can perform is to collect ideas and anecdotes from your own observations.

It's hard to find a book that can give you the answers to all your questions. Most books overstate the obvious, or they generalize about the important principles and ideas that relate to starting a new business. What I've tried to do in this book, however, is to provide you with concrete information that you can start using right away.

With that in mind, let me say that the Web is an amazing place, a virtual treasure trove of information. Moreover, established, successful websites are rich sources of marketing and sales tactics that can guide you in setting up your own business. (After all, these sites are already successful, right?)

So, in addition to the information that you'll find in this book, please be sure to check out the appendix at the end of the book. You'll find a list of websites and links that contain numerous tools and ideas for helping you launch your business.

Success in business is really just knowing how to market your product or service effectively. All of the companies profiled in this book used a variety of marketing tools and tactics to build their businesses.

Ask yourself, which of these marketing strategies would be appropriate to use for my business venture? To help you decide, think back on the different stories you've read and pay close attention to those businesses that are marketing a product or service similar to yours.

### Consider a frequent visitors program

Blink.com offers a "Blink Rewards" program, similar to an airline's frequent flyer program. You get points for clicking on the website's advertisers, which are then redeemable for goodies. In addition, this website offers visitors incentives for clicks that, in turn, help keep the site free. Incentive programs work by building loyalty and traffic.

E-Poll.com also uses a points program to get visitors to participate in its surveys. When you register, you earn points that are redeemable for prizes.

### Use affiliate marketing

Mile High Comics put up Web button on its front page to enlist and explain its associates program. Associates simply provide a link from their websites to Mile High Comics' site, and, for doing virtually nothing, they earn ten percent of the sales generated by any traffic that they drive there. Furthermore, as Web hits increase, so will the number of associates wanting to register and sign up.

Though this program is simple and easy, few are doing it—yet nearly everyone could.

### Create a brand

CarePackages.com employs an animated white bunny rabbit as its company emblem. Remember the Quik Bunny on Nestle Quik's chocolate and strawberry milk flavorings? It was one of the most recognizable brands in history, right up there with Ronald McDonald and the Coca Cola logo.

Quick, name a couple of toothpastes! Did you think of Crest or Colgate, two very recognizable brands? Branding works on the Net as well. Ask Jeeves.com has created brand recognition with its butler, who showed up in a recent Macy's Thanksgiving Day parade. Branding works.

### Use Web tools and features

Wanted Technologies provides the search engines for numerous job sites. So, right on its own website, there's a sample search box where you can take its search engine for a "test drive." The search engine works remarkably well, telling you how many jobs it found for you in how many seconds.

Web tools and features make your site useful and valuable to visitors, helping to give you the edge over your competitors. Such features give visitors something to talk about, which is actually the most powerful Web-traffic driver of all—word-of-mouth advertising.

### Place value in word-of-mouth marketing

High-volume websites don't rely on advertising, linking, or search-engine positioning alone. The bulk of their traffic is generated by word of mouth. About.com is one of the most visited sites on the Web, and it has pulled in much of its traffic through word of mouth. About.com's marketing mix is the right combination of advertising, promotion, links, branding, and general recognition of a product or service. Word of mouth is an important component of this marketing mix.

### Define your market

When you visit the site of Collages.net, you'll find there are really two niches that it serves: (1) individuals looking to place their photographs online, and (2) professional photographers, who actually comprise a distribution channel for the site. You, too, may have several market niches that could benefit from your product or service, and you should target each of those niches.

### Use the power of testimonials

Testimonials sell. If you have them, use them, and if you don't have them, get them. Nothing beats the value of an unbiased third party's good words about you, or the story of that company's success in using your product.

Visit RightNow Technologies' website, and you'll see some powerful testimonials on its front page, such as "RightNow Web Helps Pitney Bowes Save $200,000 in One Day!" and "Polaroid Enjoys a 94% Self-Service Rate with RightNow Web!" and "Social Security Administration Saves Over $16M in First Year!" Each statements is hotlinked to the page featuring the actual success story.

On seeUthere.com's front Web page, there's a button linked to its client list, plus a testimonial quote that changes each month. These are powerful uses of a marketing tool that has been proven to sell products and services for centuries!

### To build confidence, use articles and media exposure

Multicity.com has a link to an article in *Red Herring*, where the company's website is discussed, as well as

Multicity's role as an ASP (application service provider) hosting multilingual communication applications for e-commerce.

When your product or service gets press, use the clout of the third-party media by providing a hotlink to it. The publication doesn't have to be huge for it to have value. Every third-party endorsement adds to credibility.

### Think globally!

If you go to the bottom of Ask Jeeves' site, you'll see a link enabling you to ask a question in Spanish. Just this one link opens up the entire Spanish-language market, creating a new customer channel that may have been unavailable otherwise. You, too, can take advantage of inexpensive Web tools that will publish your site in several different languages. Though this tactic may not be right for you, it's well worth considering.

### Use multimedia

Visit the Feedroom.com website and you'll see what looks like a television screen, complete with streaming video and sound. It's one of the few sites I've seen that does this automatically—really neat.

If you can do the same thing on your website, you'll likely get someone to stop and listen to your message. Audio and video are currently underutilized on the Web, so they definitely get attention, resulting in a powerful impact on your sales.

### Avoid the pure play

The "pure play" is a term given to Internet and dot-com companies that rely purely on the Internet for all of their revenues. They have been touted as some of the highest-risk businesses on the Web, and I think it's safe to say that most dot-com failures have been pure plays.

To avoid the same fate, look for alternative sales channels and ways to penetrate other business niches. For example, consider an online bookstore featuring books related to your product or service, or a brick-and-mortar store, or paid subscription newsletters and market reports. You could also license your material, provide consulting services, or market your product as a corporate premium.

Think of ways to sell your product or service that don't rely on a passive Internet presence, where people must find you before they buy. And always be on the lookout for other profit centers that can sell or repackage your product or service.

Janet Attard, founder of Business Know-How, offers many things on her websites. She licenses her content to others, sells books and software, and offers advertising. In addition, she sells her own book, *The Home Office and Small Business Answer Book.*

### Don't overspend

Gil Ebaz started his search engine technology company, Oingo, with humble beginnings. Do you recall his story? He and his partners rented a large house in the Hollywood hills specifically because it had room for several them to live in, as well as space they could use for the company offices.

If you look at most dot-com failures, you'll see that these companies didn't control overhead costs. They went right for all the glitzy extras up front without easing into it. Being frugal in the early years can really pay off.

### Emulate the wisdom of others

Of the 25 entrepreneurs I interviewed, nearly all pointed to a person or book that was instrumental in shaping their ideas as they worked to get their businesses off the ground. For example, *Built to Last* by Jim Collins and Jerry Porras was inspiring to Vip Patel, founder of eHealthinsurance.com. Jeff Pledger of AbleTV.net liked *Thriving on Chaos* by Tom Peters, while Sam Alfstad, founder eMarketer.com, recommended *Competing for the Future* by Gary Hamel and C.K. Prahalad.

Others name special people as their inspiration. Scott Kurnit of About.com credits his father as a source of inspiration, and Kevin Casey of Collages.net also credits his parents. William Lam of ask dr. tech says he looked to the life of Alexander the Great for inspiration, and Jeff Pledger (AbleTV.net) was inspired by blind marathon runner Harry Cordello.

### Plan your work, work your plan

Setting milestones in a business plan sounds boring, and it's tempting to skip the planning stage when starting a business. Listen to Mary Westheimer, though, cofounder of BookZone.com: "Write a business plan. This can't be overemphasized. It's easy to bump along, but to really make progress, planning is the key."

And Ryan Moran of CarePackages.com concurs. As he puts it, "If it doesn't work on paper, it's not going to work in bricks and mortar or on the Web."

### Work hard and be persistent

Now, is this a tip? Well, it's what Jennifer Floren and many other entrepreneurs claim is a catchall tip for anyone starting *any* business.

"Dream big, but don't believe that entrepreneurial success comes from anything but persistence and hard work," says Floren. "Your small victories eventually add up to weekly and monthly progress. And, if you're lucky, that progress gets your business one step closer to success."

*A billion here,*
*a billion there, and*
*pretty soon you're talking*
*about real money.*

*— Everett Dickinson*

# Tips from Kevin Nunley

No MATTER HOW HARD I TRY, I don't think I could provide as much valuable information as Dr. Kevin Nunley does on his website. While putting together the marketing tips of the last chapter, I stumbled on www.drnunley.com—it's fantastic! This site is chock full of useful tips and advice that you can put to work immediately.

There are several marketing, small business, copywriting, and advertising persons that I admire, and Dr. Nunley is one of them. He provides powerful, useful advice for your small business and, in particular, your Web-marketing efforts. I've extracted 35 of his 10,000 tips to include in this book, but be sure to read all his free tips at http://www.drnunley.com. You can also reach Kevin at kevin@drnunley.com or (801) 253-4536.

### Have you got a meta tag?

Meta tags are the key ingredients that search engines look for when deciding how to list your website. You can't see a meta tag while looking at your page, because it's a simple code in the HTML behind your page.

Your meta tag goes near the top of your page's HTML between the <HEAD> and </HEAD> tags. Click the right mouse key (for PC users) on any good Web page, then choose "view source," and you will see the HTML code. It should look something like this:

<META NAME="description" content="Kevin Nunley—one of the Net's top business writers provides lots of tips on marketing, media, online marketing, and the Internet."><META NAME="keywords" content="marketing, advertising, ads, internet marketing, press release, copywriting, website design, small business assistance, newsletters, website promotion, selling online, e-zines, and home-based business opportunities">

This is the simple meta tag Kevin Nunley uses on his website. Some experts use fancier tags, but this one works just fine for getting you listed on search engines that emphasize meta tags. Feel free to copy it, inserting your own description and keywords.

Here's another trick. Go to a site similar to yours that ranks tops on search engines. See which keywords it's using in its meta tag and then work some of its good ideas into your own meta tag.

### Use keywords to get on search engines

Search engines are a lot smarter than they used to be. Not so long ago, what you typed into the little search box may or may not have had anything to do with the 20,000 sites the engine subsequently presented to you.

Today, search engine computers do a pretty fair job of reading through the copy on a site, then figuring out what the site is about and classifying it according to the most common keywords in the text.

For example, typing in "toothbrushes" will likely get you to a site that is all about toothbrushes rather than showing you a list of all sites mentioning toothbrushes in their texts.

Sites with lots of tightly focused information on a specific topic tend to do very well on search engines. To get a search engine's attention, try focusing intensively on a few important keywords within the first hundred words of your page.

If your site is about bicycles, make sure your text mentions the words "bicycle," "bicycles," and "bicycling," as often as is logical in good writing. It's interesting to note that search engines can detect when you're trying to cheat by using a word too much. Nonetheless, make sure the same top keywords show up in your title, in your meta tag, and in your copy.

### Don't ditch your simple website yet

Once 56K modems became the norm, many website owners figured it was time to add *lots* more graphics to their websites. One big Web design firm says its corporate clients insist on pages weighted down with custom graphics. Those sites look terrific, as long as your modem can download them quickly enough.

But, oops! There's a kink in this plan. Jupiter Communications recently announced that 78 percent of us will still be using slow dial-up telephone connections well into 2003. That means graphic-intensive websites are still ahead of their time, and most visitors will be waiting interminably for all those nifty visuals to appear.

The moral of the story—don't ditch your simple Web pages yet! Keep your pages fast loading and watch sales go up as people stick around to click through your site. To make your pages look like they have more graphics than they really do:

- Put an eye-catching logo at the top of each page.
- Use a colored bullet to set off key points in the text.

- Use colored boxes and text that load instantly.
- Repeat the same few graphics often throughout the site.

Once a graphic loads into a visitor's computer, it stays in the temporary buffer memory. Because it doesn't have to download again and again each time it appears, visitors can click almost instantly from page to page.

### Add flexibility

The most effective marketing strategy of the 1990s was to offer customers choice—in other words, flexibility. For example, think of the computer industry's trend of offering customers the option to build their own computers. This idea has become so popular with consumers that even chain computer retailers have an area where you can buy a made-to-order computer.

If you offer several different versions of your product or service, your customers will feel they have a choice. (They do!) You might also advertise that you will customize your product to suit any special needs. Not only does offering different versions of a product or service allow you to sell to a much wider market, but you may also find that this new flexibility results in a sudden leap in your sales figures.

### Watch for problems

Kevin Nunley has a little spot at the top of his website that reads: "Ask Kevin a question. Read answers to questions." People ask him for answers to lots of different problems. Though he may not always know the answer (he claims his batting average has been pretty poor lately), he sure gets to know what issues are plaguing his visitors.

No doubt you hear about customer problems all day, too. But, do you realize that for every problem, there is a customer who will pay you to solve that problem? Maybe you could solve it with a service, a recommendation, or a product.

When people consistently come to you with the same problems, you've got a terrific opportunity to build a new profit stream. Don't assume that somebody is already selling solutions for all the world's great problems. Think a minute or two about the big stumpers in your biz, and you'll likely discover several annoyances that nobody seems to be working on.

For instance, survey after survey shows that people in my town love ice cream, but we have very few places to buy a great ice cream cone. Or what about the dozen or so bookstores in my town—all of them are located in the same area. And it seems each block has a half dozen businesses that would love to be on the Internet, but they don't have a clue how to go about it.

Does anybody see an opportunity for income here?

### Tell about your failures

Can you tell a story about how you tried and failed— sometimes many times—before finally succeeding? Most of us have such stories. Believe it or not, your bumpy-road-to-success story is one of the most powerful marketing tools around.

Your story doesn't have to be an impressive one, but average people should be able to identify with it. It could be about a problem that dogged your business or workplace before you finally found the solution. Customers and prospects love and remember these stories.

Rags-to-riches stories play extremely well on the Internet. Jim Daniels is widely known for the story of how he went from a frustrated middle manager to an Internet mogul. People identify with his early failed attempts at starting his own business, and they are encouraged by how he triumphed to earn a good living online.

Tell your story in a bio, a press release, or an "our story" Web page. Show how you started with difficult odds, worked hard, took your ups and downs, and finally achieved success.

### Send a fan letter to an expert in your field

People love to get notes from others who admire their work. A fan letter can open doors, create relationships, and get insider information fast. Even famous people like getting notes from admirers. Many big egos thrive on fan letters and figure their careers are faltering if they are not getting them.

You can send your note via regular mail or email. Start by mentioning how you have followed his or her work and found it interesting, important, or helpful. Then add your own ideas to show you are also involved in the subject or issue. Finally, ask a question. Give the reader a reason to respond to your message, and provide several ways to respond. Many busy professionals love super-convenient email. Others will fax you a letter. Yet others will pick up the phone and call you!

Warning—be polite, be brief, don't get too pushy, and *never* try to sell them anything in the first contact.

### Letter to the editor

Many newspapers, magazines, and industry publications print letters from readers. Your letter to the editor can be a good way to get exposure in a big publication, but make sure it doesn't read like an ad for your business. Otherwise, it won't get printed.

Instead, use your letter to let lots of readers know that you are someone with inside information, or that you have an interesting view or a solution to a problem.

Also, your letter carries a better chance of being printed if it is about an issue that was recently covered by the publication. Compliment the author of the article for a doing a good job in reporting the story, then add your comments. Kevin says he's used this technique over and over—editors love it!

A friend who has a weekly commentary feature on a local radio station managed to get his letter printed in *Newsweek*, which significantly raised his standing in the eyes of his local listeners. You could get the same kind of benefit by sending a letter to the main trade publication in your industry.

Sometimes you can strike a chord with readers, and many of them will send in letters either agreeing with you, disagreeing with you, or furthering the argument. In this way, you could get mentioned again and again in the publication, sometimes for weeks or even months.

### Make yourself famous in discussion groups

Being an expert can really capture sales. When people know you can help their situation with experience and knowledge, they don't mind paying for whatever you suggest.

One of the Net's best tools for turning yourself into a recognized expert in your field is by participating in discussion groups. These can be Usenet newsgroups (check with your Internet service provider for how to find them), or they can be discussion groups on websites. There are also email discussion groups, sometimes called listservs or majordomos.

Pick no more than two or three groups in which to participate. Join the groups, but just hide and watch for a while. Get to know what kinds of topics are discussed and who the main characters are. Many groups have at least one "troll under the bridge," who seems to thrive on running down anyone who takes a different viewpoint.

Once you have a feel for the group, be the one who can give a good solid answer to a given question. Then, make it your goal to answer a question this way once or twice each week. Keep your answer strictly noncommercial, but be sure to include your commercial signature file at the end of your response. That way, people will have your email address and know where to find your website.

Several successful business folks have told me that their only method of advertising was participation in discussion groups. They say it generated many a customer over a period of months.

### What to put in your autoresponders

Free autoresponders are everywhere, and we've all heard about what a powerful, effortless tool they are for follow-up selling. After all, most customers won't buy the first time. They only buy if you remind them to buy.

With this in mind, try writing an information "article" to put in your autoresponder. I put "article" in quotations because you don't have to write a regular magazine or newspaper article.

I know a man who does very well with a series of top-ten lists—the top ten ways to get on a search engine or the top ten ways to get visitors to your order form. It could just as easily be the top ten ways to improve the look of your yard.

The key is to zero in on a specific, precise audience that is deeply interested in a particular issue. Your autoresponder article could offer news about your new project or service. Explain why you developed it, how it works, why folks are using it, what benefit it brings, and how the reader can get a special deal.

Courses are also good. People love to get a seven-lesson course on a popular topic. It can be delivered to them each day, or every other day, or once a week. Such courses will keep you on their mind for days, weeks, or even months—until the sale comes in.

### How to get testimonials

Nothing sells products and services like positive comments from past customers. Prospects will believe the word of a customer long before they'll buy into even the best-written ad or most lavish TV commercial. But how do you get good testimonials, especially if your business is new?

Well, nobody says *you* can't provide the testimonial. If you have personally used the product you are selling and truly believe it's the best thing since sliced bread, put that in a testimonial with your own words in quotations.

You can also get someone who is a recognized name in your field to say something good about what you sell. Let them mention their own interest in the testimonial. This is why blurbs on book covers go, "Best book I've ever read," Joe Blow, author of *How to Get Rich*. Joe lends his good opinion as a way to get a mention for *his* book.

Another way to generate testimonials is to put up a comments form on your website. State clearly that some comments may be selected for display on your site or in your promotional literature. Some people will say good things (sincerely, of course) just to get their names in print. Always include the person's first and last name along with his home town or the business he works for. Otherwise, people will think you made up the testimonial.

### Promote your USP

Your USP is your "unique selling position." It's the one thing you have that your competitors don't. Your USP could be a product or service that people want but that others don't sell. Or if you all have the same products, point out how your products are original, one of a kind, or first to market. What makes you special?

Your USP could also be something intangible, such as friendly service in a notoriously unfriendly service environment. (Auto repair or the dry cleaner?) One search engine promotion firm I worked with never answered email, while another always replied within hours. There's no question which company gets my business.

Whatever it is, promoting your USP helps to get you more customers. So, put your unique selling position on your business card, in your newspaper ads, and front-and-center on your website. If all the businesses in your industry keep their prices a big secret, for example, publish yours right out in the open where anyone can see. You'd be surprised how many of us won't buy if we have to ask what the price is.

### Quick ways to get more visitors to your site

Can you use a quick boost in website visitors as you go into the holiday shopping season? Here's how to do it:

- **Offer free software to your customers.**
  Check out tucows.com to find software developers eager to distribute their work for free.

- **Offer a free course via email.**
  Your course need only consist of a few informative pages that help your target customers solve a common problem.

- **Offer to help or answer questions at no charge.**
  Kevin Nunley's offer to look at a website and offer an opinion always draws lots of response.

- **Start your own contest.**
  Make sure you have lots of small-prize winners, making each eligible to win a much larger prize in the future.

- **Write a press release about all the special promotions you're doing.**
  Put it on its own Web page, and then register it with Alta Vista, Excite, Yahoo, and Hot Bot. Use Kevin's free press announcement builder at http:// InternetWriters.com/release.htm.

### Two top reasons why marketing fails

Ads sometimes don't work. There are a lot of reasons why this happens, but more often than not, we can point to two downfalls that seem to hurt marketing.

Problem one is that your ad isn't clear to the people it is aimed at. Most of us have words and phrases we use in our industry that make little sense to our customers. Strive to put your ideas in plain everyday language. Translate your industry buzz words into words that everyone uses.

Lots of times, the one important benefit that will make people buy gets lost somewhere in the copy. For example, when I get a long email message from someone, they'll often have the important part in the next-to-last paragraph. If I were in a hurry, I wouldn't see it.

Problem two is that marketing isn't directed at the right people. One guy who wanted to recruit members for his MLM opportunity advertised in the daily newspaper. Lots of people read the paper, but few were interested in network marketing. Putting his ad in a networking publication or e-zine that reached his target audience would have served him much better.

### Full-color postcards

Postcards are the direct marketer's ace in the hole. They are cheaper to send than regular letters, and people can read them without having to open an envelope, which is a *huge* advantage. Many experienced direct mail marketers say full-color postcard campaigns get double the response of a sales letter at only half the price.

Printing firms that specialize in postcards typically offer full-color cards for about $100 per 1,000 cards. Full-color cards practically jump out of a prospect's stack of mail. Don't you reach first for the exotic full-color postcard sent by a vacationing relative? Your cards can have the same attention-getting power.

Try to have your photo or graphic help tease the message on the back. Use a headline to deliver your main offer, and include a time limit to increase the response rate. One smart marketer sends monthly postcards to his customers that include his message plus a photo that he's taken on his vacations.

### Market with your order form

Your customers lead busy lives and may not always remember what they did and where. For example, when I worked in radio, we were amazed at how often people couldn't remember from which station they had won a prize. You'll run into this situation yourself. People may buy from you, then forget whom they bought from just a few weeks later. That's a real problem if you are depending on word of mouth—which you should!

Therefore, be sure to put your bright and bold logo on every one of your order forms. This tactic will stamp your name onto your customer's memory at the time of the sale.

Some smart businesspeople have actually turned their order form into a brochure. They place an ad and a full list of their products and services in the brochure, then put the order form on the final page. A brochure also gives you extra space to include a coupon for the next purchase.

### FREE Internet ads

Free Internet classifieds are everywhere. There are literally thousands of sites that let you post an ad of 25 to 100 words at no charge. If you're willing to be a little bit clever and roll up your sleeves, you can reach an amazing number of prospects without spamming.

Is this a magic weapon? Unfortunately, no. You see, because these promotional tools are free, *everyone* uses them. So, getting your ad noticed is about the same as shouting your message from the bleachers right after a touchdown at the Super Bowl. However, you can increase your chances of being noticed by adding sizzling marketing words to your subject line, such as *free, new, powerful, save, profit, free computer*, or *big money*. These are some of the eye-catching words that work the best.

You'll also want to use Peter Theill's free software to help you post your ads quickly (http://www.theill.com). Folks also have good luck using the Power Submitter at becanada.com. These programs and others will post your ad to hundreds of sites at blinding speed.

### Get listed on Yahoo

Yahoo is by far the most popular search engine on the Internet. In fact, a simple listing on Yahoo can boost hits to your site by 2,000 per day.

The only problem is that Yahoo still individually inspects each proposed index addition and lists only a small fraction of the sites that are submitted. However, Robin Nobles of http://www.academywebspecialists.com/ has some insider advice on how to get listed.

First of all, Yahoo likes link pages—pages with lots of links to other websites—so consider adding one to your site. Next, the relevancy score for Yahoo appears to be based on the category followed by the title, description, and URL. If your website is tied to a particular event or current news where time is of the essence, you may have an easier time getting in the index.

What else? If you have a regionally specific site, consider submitting it in that area. Regional submissions sometimes have an easier time getting in because those editors don't have quite as many submissions. Also, submitting to a category that doesn't have too many entries may help you get in faster as well.

Also, if you're trying to get a second domain listed for the same company, make sure you use different contact information and present it in a new and unique way in a different category. Don't link back and forth between the first domain and the second. Keep them totally separate until they're indexed. Then you can go back and link them together with no problem.

### Press release myths

Lots of experts like to tell you what to do and what not to do in a press release. Most of their advice is excellent, but it seems there are a few insider tips they are missing. Recently a PR expert wrote to Kevin Nunley and advised him to stop telling people to use press releases. "The media is so busy that a press release is the last thing they have time for," she said.

On the other hand, most media folks are constantly looking for good stories and information, and they don't care how they get it. Even though media people get too much mail, too many phone calls, and an avalanche of email, they are always short of great stories.

Another press release maxim instructs you not to call an editor and ask if he or she received your press release. True, this is at the top of many editors' pet peeve lists, but no one gets anywhere in the media without being persistent.

In fact, media folks move up into prestigious organizations and high-paying jobs by calling and emailing prospective bosses over and over. Find a media pro with an impressive track record, and you'll likely find someone who is a real pest when shooting for a new job.

Bottom line—be persistent and you'll be there when an editor, writer, producer, or reporter finally decides there's a need for your story.

### Increase sales with autoresponders

Kevin recently discovered an interesting trick to boost website sales. Locate an email box right below the offer for your product or service and just below the button people need to click on to place an order. The box should say: "Would you like more information? Put your email address in the box, and we will send it to you." Then have the form trigger a series of three autoresponder messages.

Each message should tell the customer more about your offer, the benefits it can bring them, and other helpful information. You'll be amazed at how well this method works.

We found that almost half of those who asked for more information purchased the product or service shortly thereafter. That's because only ten percent of us are true impulse buyers, yet most websites focus on getting the visitor to buy *now*. The fact is that most people need time to consider a purchase before they will give out their credit card information.

Another way to use an autoresponder is to send out a brief series of messages, one arriving each day. It's a terrific way to keep your prospects interested and thinking about you. In the messages, include links to your site and to the specific page that features the offer. In most email programs, putting http:// before your URL will turn it into a live link that customers can click on.

### New longer domain names

Your domain name (yourname.com) can now be 67 characters long. Yikes! I thought, when I first heard of this. Many domain names are already too long to remember, so what are we going to do with names that are more than twice as long? It turns out there are three good answers to that question.

One, you may need a longer domain to spell out your business's full name—JimBobs-Emporium-AutoParts-CommunityCollege-and Pizzaria.com.

Two, you can use a well-known sentence or phrase for your domain name. Just like the techniques country music songwriters use, people will be able to remember your phrase. For example:

DoesMyRingHurtYourFingerWhenYouGo
OutAtNight.com  (catchy, huh?)

Three, you can list your most important keywords in your domain name. Search engines tend to rank sites higher if the word people are searching with is included in the site's domain name.

### Include step-by-step details

Prospects and customers love it when you give them step-by-step directions. Really. You'll find that your sales will soar when your marketing materials tell customers what you want them to do. Tell them *how* you want them to do it and never leave them asking, "What do I do next?"

A large segment of customers will buy from you if your headline starts with: "Step-by-step details that show anyone how to do (whatever) easily." Limit your steps to three to five, if possible, because lists of ten steps or more can be intimidating.

Assure customers you are there to help them as they follow your list of to-do's. Provide an email address or phone number where they can get information quickly, and point them to a spot on your website that can help them through the process. In addition, this spot should include stories of how other customers successfully followed your instructions.

The step-by-step strategy can also work with a slightly different twist. Try giving customers a step-by-step list of exactly what *you* will do when providing your service or delivering a product. Such information sets your customers at ease and gives them confidence that they will get a good value on their purchase. It also greatly reduces the number of questions you have to answer via email and over the phone.

### Get more response from email

Tens of millions of people use email every day. It is now by far the most popular feature of the Internet. Many successful entrepreneurs have found they can do business with nothing more than an email address. Here are some simple ways to get better response from email messages.

- Target your message. Response always goes up when you send your message to someone who is likely to respond. That's why it's vital to build your own opt-in list of people who have already said they want your information.

- Personalize your message. Prospects respond better when your message uses their name, and response goes up even higher when your message refers to their particular situation and offers a relevant solution.

- Use a little HTML coding in your email address. Typing in "mailto:" before your email address makes it a live, clickable link on many email programs. Rather than typing your address into their email program, prospects can act on impulse and simply click your link.

- Keep in mind that 60 percent of us don't type, and many more of us don't type very well or don't like to type. Again, you can increase response by placing the HTML code just mentioned in front of your email address, like so:

  mailto:you@YourAddress.com?subject=Send_Me_Info

  This way, your prospect doesn't have to type anything to send a message. "Send Me Info" automatically shows up as the subject in the email response.

## Three-letter autoresponder follow-up

Recently, a woman told Kevin, "Your advertising is wasted if you don't follow up on your leads." She suggested using a multiple autoresponder to send new prospects a different sales message every few days.

Also, we learned in the last few pages that people need to see an ad message several times before they'll buy. In fact, those who appear to buy on the first ad have likely already made up their minds due to seeing someone else's ad earlier. Your ad simply had the good fortune of reaching that customer at just the right time.

You can greatly increase your sales in both of these situations by using a three-letter multiple autoresponder, and there are a number of places to get them for free. Fastfacts.net, getresponse.com, and smartbotpro.com all offer free autoresponders, and you'll find other businesses selling upgraded services at a low cost.

The first letter should present your offer briefly. It should be designed to get attention and bring in those buyers who tend to make up their minds quickly.

The second sales letter should then arrive the next day, and it should be longer and filled with details. That's because about 70 percent of us consumers are folks who need *all* the details before we'll purchase. In your letter, first list the outstanding features of your product or service and then connect those features with the benefits your customers can expect to receive.

Your third sales letter should be scheduled to arrive several days later. Start it with: "Successful people are busy. I know you probably saw my earlier messages and considered them, but haven't yet had time to respond." Now it's time to present your offer again, but be sure to bring in a fresh angle. You don't want your prospects to think they're reading the same letter they got a few days ago.

More than three sales letters tend to get ignored. If you want to send more, have your fourth and fifth letters arrive weeks or months later. Scheduling a new letter to arrive every month, for example, can sometimes catch a prospect when he or she is ready to buy.

### Hot new search engine trick

Jerry West works full-time as a search engine expert for several big e-commerce companies. (See Jerry's free search engine guide at http://WebMarketingNow.com/.) He has a smart new strategy that could quickly boost business for all of us.

His method revolves around building a few pages for your site that contain exactly those items the search engine Ask Jeeves is looking for. The following five simple steps increased Jerry's hits by almost 40 percent.

1. Think of a question or two that customers ask you again and again. In my line, people ask, "Where can I get cheap ads?" and "How can I send out a press release?"

   These are the kinds of questions lots of people ask Ask Jeeves.

2. Put your question in the title of your page. (The title is the line that shows up in the little box on your browser.)

3. Put the answer to your question in the description area of your meta tag. (See AltaVista.com's "submit URL" page for a good explanation of how to do this.)

4. Write your question as a big headline at the top of your Web page. Then go on to discuss the question and its answer on your page and include links to the main pages of your website.

5. Last, you'll need to register your question page with AltaVista.com, Excite.com, HotBot.com, and DirectHit.com. These are the search engines that Ask Jeeves looks through as it compiles an answer to a visitor's question.

### Fast-loading pages

As browsers become more sophisticated and modems are able to download faster, websites are getting fancier. On the other hand, many website visitors still have slow, dial-up phone lines with no near-term improvement planned.

For fast-loading pages, Kevin's old advice was to put a logo at the top of your Web page and keep the remainder of the page for text. But as Web design grows ever more complex, people's expectations tend to follow. The resulting contradiction has put many of us between a rock and a hard place.

Nonetheless, here are some ways to jazz up the look of your Web pages without bogging them down:

- Use one to three small .gif or .jpeg graphics on a page, but don't go overboard. Once a graphic has downloaded into a visitor's computer, it doesn't have to download again, so try to repeat graphics from one page to the next.

- Create an interesting page by formatting your text. You can use headlines, bold text, indented blocks,

and limited color text. You can also set off important points with small graphic balls or arrows. These
don't take much time to load and can add interest to
your page.

- Group parts of your page in a cell with a different
  background from the rest of your page.

### "But, we tried everything!"

Occasionally, Kevin Nunley is consulted by a business
that has done a ton of marketing, but still isn't selling
much. It's not for lack of effort, though. On the con-
trary—the list of attempted marketing strategies is usually staggering.

So, if thousands, or even millions, of prospects are learning about a product or service, why aren't any of them
buying? Here are some common reasons why even well-
promoted products don't sell.

- **There isn't any real market for the product.**
  It may seem like a great idea, but nobody wants it—
  at least, not yet.

- **Customers don't think your business is qualified
  to sell the product.**
  One man knew his medium-sized business could supply the needs of major customers, but they didn't
  buy until his company grew into a big corporation.
  "We could have served them just as well before, but
  they wouldn't buy because they thought we weren't
  big enough," he said.

- **Your advertising isn't targeted at the right market.**
  This is probably the most common problem. A company may market through media that reaches a mass
  audience, such as TV or daily newspapers, but find

that too few of its potential customers are exposed to this type of media.

Tightly targeted media doesn't always reach the audience it claims to reach. Before spending big bucks, try running a test first to see if you get results.

### Promote with auction sites

Need a quick way to boost your website traffic? If the number of hits on your site is a bit depressing, you might want to try an auction. Jerry West, the Internet marketing expert we met earlier, says some sites have found that online auctions can boost their traffic. (Read Jerry's free online marketing manual at WebMarketingNow.com.)

This is how it works. First you list a product or service at far below its actual worth. Then set up ad copy and a link to your site on a bidding screen. Jerry has seen as many as 400 visitors click to the bidding screen, with an average of about 65 hits.

An auction is a good, cost-effective means of bringing targeted traffic to your site. As long as your page does a good job of covering the product or service listed on the auction site, you will get lots of inquiries.

Of course, this is one of the oldest tricks around, well known to retailers as "loss leaders." Watch what happens when a big department store in your area advertises a popular product at a very low price. The store may be losing money on the featured item, but it gets plenty of customers into the store who may well buy other products that are not discounted.

### Creative opt-in lists

Email is currently the Internet's most popular tool. It's also a terrific way to market your products and services.

However, sending email to people you don't know is prohibited by law in many places and discouraged everywhere (i.e., spam). So, businesses are now pursuing new prospects with "opt-in" email.

Opt-in lists are made up of people who have asked to be on the list. Advertising sent to opt-in lists tends to be very effective and rarely causes the problems associated with spamming. There are a number of good opt-in list services, such as bulletmail.com, targ-it.com, and postmasterdirect.com/.

Such lists can be quite expensive, running up to 25 cents per name and requiring large minimum purchases. But, there are also low-cost opt-in lists hiding all over the Net. For example, many e-zines have big lists of dedicated subscribers. Try asking the publisher to put your sales letter or press release in a special issue.

Other sites offer popular reports and courses via multi-message autoresponders and then compile legitimate opt-in lists from the people who subscribe. You can do this yourself by advertising a hot report or e-book on your site. Just make sure that the people who request it agree to let you send them more information in the future.

Above all, make sure opt-in lists really *are* opt-in. There are a lot of "safe" lists being offered that are made up of addresses found on newsgroups and in classified ads. If someone accuses you of spamming, you will want to produce proof that the person opted to be on the list.

### Rich text email letters

You've got your sales letter all set to go. It's typed up beautifully in Word, complete with headlines, bullets, and bold text. There's no question that you're holding a brilliant selling machine in your hands.

Now try to email your letter to a customer. If you attach your letter, a customer is likely to write back that she got nothing but a page of code. "Your letter was all scrambled," she replies.

Hmm . . . apparently she doesn't have a compatible word processing program. So, you copy and paste your sales letter into the body of the email, but then all the fancy formatting you worked so hard on is lost.

Well, here's a cure—or at least a partial cure—for scrambled sales letters. Save your letter as a "rich text file" and then attach it to your email. You'll find rich text options in the "Save As" selections that your word processor offers you.

In most cases, a letter in rich text will transmit fine over the Internet. It will also open in most word processors with your headlines and other formatting intact. This works so well that I rarely mail or fax a sales letter anymore. I simply attach it as a rich text file.

### Working with virtual partners

If you need help running your Internet business or the online side of your offline business, consider getting a virtual partner.

These folks are capable people who excel in some area of online business. Typically, they're willing to work for a cut of your sales or for the referrals they can get for their own companies. Keep in mind, though, that they are not traditional partners who own a share of your firm.

There are many ways to utilize a virtual partner, whether on a contract or commission basis. Most importantly, though, he or she can help you solve the very real problem of not having enough time to run your business.

For instance, Kevin mentions that he no longer has time to design websites for people, yet many of his customers want him to write the copy for their sites. His solution was to develop virtual partnerships with several very capable designers, who take his copy and whip it up into flashy Web pages. Customers are delighted with great work that Kevin wouldn't have been able to give them on his own.

### Why isn't my site listed on search engines yet?

You've put up a new website, gotten all your meta tag info and copy ready, and registered your site with all the major search engines. Then you sit back and wait for your listing to show up in countless searches that will drive thousands of eager buyers to your pages. And you wait, and you wait, and you wait.

Be patient, and don't get too obsessive. The fact is, the exploding backlog of new websites has become far more than search engines can handle. You can expect to wait months to get listed on Yahoo, if you can listed at all.

However, a few of the major search engines now have superfast indexing technology that can have your site up within a few days to two weeks. Among these are Infoseek, AltaVista, and HotBot.

Once sites are listed on the six or seven major search engines, they tend to start showing up on many other search engines and link libraries. You can register your site with all the major engines with one click at http://www.all4one.com/. You can also register free with over 400 search engines and link libraries at http://www.submit4free.com/.

Search engine technology is constantly changing. For the latest tips check http://www.searchenginewatch.com/.

This site is widely regarded as the Net's best source of up-to-the-minute search engine info.

### Niching with different website entry pages

One reader asked Kevin why some Web promotion experts suggest you should never send people directly to your website's opening page. Always send them to an entry page, they say. Why? The answer is that by having different entry pages, you can customize your look and copy for specific groups of people.

Let's say you sell products to the general public, but you also solicit people to distribute your products for a cut of the profits. The headlines and copy you use to interest a product customer will probably be quite different from the way you pitch to someone who might be interested in your business opportunity.

Different entry pages also allow you to get more search engine action. Most search engines favor sites that have a lot of information on a specific, narrowly defined subject.

One big mystery, though, is why so many sites have an entry page that is nothing more than a big graphic with a link to the main page. That seems like a big waste of a good marketing opportunity. Your entry pages should clearly tell readers what you can offer them. Give them some exciting copy right away, and don't make them click through several pages to find out what benefits you offer.

### Get more response with simple forms

After putting together a website with lots of helpful information and a strong sales message, you write at the bottom of the page: "Email me for more info or to order." But when you check the number of people who are visiting your website, you see that only a small fraction are sending you email.

You can increase your email response by replacing your "mail to" link with a simple form. For some reason, when presented with fill-in-the-blank boxes, people are far more likely to type their name, email address, and a short response. To build your own forms quickly and easily, go to http://www.freedback.com/ and http://www.response-o-matic.com/. All of these forms can be customized and run on free websites.

You'll also want to download a free copy of John Orfali's popular IO Wizard at http://iowizard.com/. This program lets you design all kinds of forms with an easy interface similar to a word processor.

### Email your press release—get free publicity

I'm going to contradict an earlier tip, now, by saying that the media *thrives* on press releases, but what I really mean is that they need *good stories*. Over half of the news you read in business publications comes from press releases (stories!) sent to them by businesses and organizations.

The media world is intensely competitive, but all—TV stations, radio, newspapers, and networks—have had to scale back and tighten budgets. The result is that they rely more than ever on the stories you send them, and a newsworthy press release means lots of free media coverage for your business.

Send your release to the media via email, because almost everyone in media uses email. And make sure your story is something the media audience will be interested in hearing about. Editors hate getting a release that is nothing more than an ad in disguise. To learn how to format a press release, check out the samples at drnunley.com.

There are several good email release services that have long lists of media contacts. For example, Memail.com recently paid $225 for Xpresspress.com to send a release to its list. The press release received major network coverage, and Memail.com picked up thousands of new subscribers in a single weekend.

If you look around a little bit, you can find even lower rates. At http://www.gapent.com/pr, a minimum order is just $50. But if you find yourself sending out lots of releases, consider getting a media list and sending them yourself. Gebbieinc.com has a terrific media guide and lots of free media addresses listed on its site.

*Victory belongs to the most persevering.*

*— Napoleon Bonaparte*

# Build a Better Website

CAN YOU READ THROUGH a few more pages? I certainly hope so, because I believe this last section of advice may be more important than almost anything else I've written about so far.

Much like traditional business brochures and other marketing materials, the way you set up your website reflects strongly on your business. It's no accident that the art of designing a good website has become a whole new branch of graphic design. So, whether you design the site yourself or hire professionals to do it, be sure to build a website that your visitors will appreciate.

Here are some specific ideas to keep in mind:

### Define your audience and what they're after

Early in the process of creating your website, identify who your current and targeted users are and why they would come to your site.

You'll need this information to clarify your website objectives, and it will help you determine your priorities as well the site's page designs.

### Provide multiple paths to information

Give your users alternative ways to get to the information they need. For example, offer a search engine in addition to menu pages.

### Make the site as "flat" as possible

Lead users to information in as few mouse clicks as you possibly can.

### Provide global navigation on each page

Users may arrive in the middle of your site, so be sure to tell them what else you have to offer.

### Text navigation is preferable to graphics

Text navigation works better than icons, pictures, or graphics because it gives you the opportunity to explain or describe the content.

### Create a search function

Sites larger than 100 pages should augment their navigation aids with a search tool. The keyword search box or search form that users complete to perform a search must be clear and easy to use.

Use terminology that matches your users' terminology, and provide simple instructions and tools to help guide them through the search.

### Make links clear

Make it clear where each link leads. Users navigate more successfully and are more likely to select a link when they can predict where it will lead.

### Use text links

Website visitors look at text links first. Because graphic links are generally less descriptive, they may be overlooked or misunderstood by users.

### Describe linked content

Each link should be simple and clear. If the link is not descriptive enough as is, provide a brief description of the linked page.

### Provide a table of contents for longer pages

If you must make a page longer than two or three screens, provide a table of contents at the top of the page.

### Clearly identify links to other sites

When you link to another website, let users know. They need to know when they are leaving your pages.

### Include a site map

Users who have access to site maps are much more successful in finding what they need than users who don't. Caution—your site map must be accurate and up to date.

### Minimize the number of colors you use

Fewer colors equals a shorter download time, and choose browser-safe colors. Only 216 colors appear consistently on all platforms (PC and Mac) and browsers.

Also, be careful about your selection of colors—in some cultures, for example, black or red may represent death!

### Be consistent

If you must vary the appearance of different sections of your website, keep the look and feel of the navigational elements consistent. Changes may confuse users.

### Use subheads to break up information

Help users to easily find information on your pages by providing subheads in lengthy text.

### Limit page length to two or three screens, if possible

Some documents need to be longer than two or three screens, sometimes much longer. If so, provide within-page navigation, such as a table of contents at the top of the page. New studies show that users are more willing to scroll than they used to be.

### Use a light background
White is best, but very light colors also work. Provide high contrast between the text and the background.

### Promote high-priority areas
Promote areas you want to make sure users see, either by placing them prominently or making them larger than the surrounding elements.

### Use your logo on each page
Visitors may arrive at any page on your site from a search engine or directory, such as Yahoo or AltaVista. A logo provides a point of reference.

### Link to your home page
Provide a way to get back to your central navigation when the user is elsewhere in the site.

### No need for complete sentences
Complete sentences may not be necessary. Increase users' ability to scan by reducing redundancy and eliminating words that do not add meaning.

### Use bullets and lists to help users scan
If you must use paragraphs, make them short with one idea in each. Text formatted this way is easier to read.

### Avoid using all capitals
Text in a combination of upper and lower case is much easier to scan.

### Font size 12 is best
This is the font size most users can read easily.

### Keep illustrative graphics simple and small
For informational sites, use graphics only to enhance navigation or to illustrate content.

# A Few Last Words

YOUR WEBSITE IS YOUR company's gateway to the world. It is, in fact, your virtual storefront, and the ease with which a prospect can navigate your website directly determines how often he or she visits as well as the length of each visit. Hopefully, all the preceding advice will help you to build the best website for your company that you possibly can.

As I began this section on marketing, I cautioned you that you can never stop learning. I want to emphasize that fact again, and I also want to offer my support and encouragement for all the efforts you are making in that direction.

Finally, it is my sincere wish that this book will help you to pursue your dream of an Internet business. I look forward to visiting you on the Web!

# Appendix

HERE'S MY LITTLE BLACK BOOK of links that were good . . . as of yesterday, at least.

Well, you know what I mean. Links don't last forever, but here are some good ones that can help you help yourself. Whether you're just starting out or you're a seasoned pro, there's bound to be at least one you never knew about.

## BUSINESS (SMALL)

### Business Plans

www.business-plan.com/realworld.htm
www.businessplanguides.com/
www.bplans.com/
www.bizplanit.com/
www.businessplans.org/
www.dotcomplans.com/
www.morebusiness.com/
www.bulletproofbizplans.com/
www.howtowritebusinessplans.com/
www.realbusinessplans.com/
www.growthink.com/
www.abconsulting.net/
www.planmaker.com/
www.venplan.com/
www.ebusinesstutor.com/

### Businesses for Sale

www.mergernetwork.com/
www.bizbuysell.com/
www.business4u.com/
www.bbn-net.com/
www.bizquest.com/
www.boj.com/
www.webbsales.net/
www.franchise-update.com/
www.brokerpages.com/
www.businessesforsale.com/
www.wholesaledistributionbusinessesforsale.com/
www.relocatablebusinessesforsale.com/
www.retailrelatedbusinessesforsale.com/
www.manufacturingbusinessesforsale.com/
www.bizsale.com/
www.ibizseller.com/
www.businessesforsaleonline.com/
www.nationwidebusinesses.com/

### General Info

www.businessfinance.com/sbdc.asp
www.sba.gov/
www.score.org
www.ideasiteforbusiness.com/
www.entrepreneur.com/
www.benlore.com/
www.smallbizmail.com/
www.bloomberg.com/business/
www.entrepreneur-web.com/
www.entrepreneur-america.com/
www.aentrepreneur.com/
http://www.hoaa.com/
http://www.edgeonline.com/
http://www.financenet.gov/
http://www.incorporate.com/

### General Info (continued)

www.bizroadmap.com/
www.theiea.org/
www.entrepreneurstoolbox.com/
www.efficient-entrepreneur.net/
worldentre.com/
www.educatedentrepreneur.com/
www.planetentrepreneur.com/
www.entrepreneurmom.com/
www.ezwww.com/
www.house.gov/smbiz/

## DIRECT MARKETING

### Direct Marketing

www.the-dma.org/
http://www.eletter.com/
http://www.directmedia.com/
www.dmworld.com/
www.dmplaza.com/
www.marketingclick.com/
www.targetonline.com/
www.direct-marketing.org/
http://www.edmarketing.com/

### Direct Marketing Lists and List Brokers

http://www.leadgreed.com/
http://www.mediasynergy.com/
http://www.nationwidedata.com/
http://www.edithroman.com/
http://www.prospectsinfluential.com/
http:/www.ozvoxmedia.com/
emaillistbrokersservices.htm
http://www.mailking.com/

## FINANCIAL

### Account Management
www.checkfree.com/
www.psigate.com/
www.cybersource.com/
http://merchantcommerce.net/
www.verisign.com/
www.merchantexpress.com/
www.paypal.com/

### Health Insurance and Benefits
http://www.e-benefits.com/
www.nase.org/
www.ehealthinsurance.com
bizbenefits.com/
www.insure.com/business/
www.businessweek.com/smallbiz/

### Intellectual Property
www.ipmag.com/
www.ipmall.fplc.edu/
www.wipo.org/
www.ipcenter.com/
www.aipla.org/
www.ipo.org/
www.delphion.com/
www.intelproplaw.com/
www.iipa.com/

### Loans and Lenders for Small Business
www.moneyzone.com/
www.nvca.org/
www.vfinance.com/
http://www.smallbusinessloans.com/

### Loans and Lenders (continued)
www.smallbizlending.com/
http://www.equalfooting.com/
businessphilosophy.com/

## FOR FREE

### Free Classified Ad Sites
www.freeclassifieds.com/
www.comcorner.com/
classifieds.yahoo.com/
www.classifieds2000.com/
www.1second.com/

### Miscellaneous Free Stuff
www.thefreesite.com/
www.freestuffcenter.com/
www.totallyfreestuff.com/
www.nojunkfree.com/
www.freestuffpage.com/
www.freestuffshare.com/
www.freestuffhq.com/

### Submit Free Articles About Your Businesss
http://www.boconline.com/
http://list-news.com/
http://www.iboost.com/promote/reciprocal_marketing/
       content/00583.htm
http://www.ideamarketers.com/
http://www.lrsmarketing.com/Resources/
       free_articles.htm
http://www.mediapeak.com/
http://list-resources.com/s/Content/Articles/
http://www.marketing-seek.com/articles/index.shtml

## MARKETING

### Affiliate Marketing and Link Building
www.linkshare.com/
www.affiliatemarketing.co.uk/
www.i-revenue.net/
www.clickz.com/
www.affiliatehandbook.com/
www.affiliateprimer.com/
www.affiliatetips.com/
www.affiliatehelp.com/
http://affiliatemarketingcouk.cj.com/
www.eliteaffiliates.com/
www.reciprocallink.com/
http://associate-it.com/Marketing/
www.drnunley.com/
http://www.ozvoxmedia.com/

### Fulfillment Services
www.dotcomdist.com/
www.prafulfillment.com/
www.dotcomdist.com
www.issidata.com/
www.gfsinc.com/
www.bizfulfillment.com/
www.qfsinc.com/
http://www.owd.com/

### Marketing and Public Relations
www.wilsonweb.com/
cyberatlas.internet.com/
www.promotion101.com/
www.effectivewebmarketing.com/
www.webmarketingnow.com/
www.webcmo.com/
www.prweb.com/
www.webpr.co.uk/

### Marketing and Public Relations (continued)
www.online-pr.com/
www.buildingchannels.com/
http://sites.krislyn.com/pr.htm
www.odwyerpr.com/
www.online-pr.com/
http://www.pr2.com/
http://www.marketitright.com/

### Permission Marketing
www.permission.com/
http://www.jimnovo.com/
http://www.kerndirect.com/pmarketing.htm
www.yesmail.com/
www.inboxexpress.com/
www.permissionmarketing.ws/

## MEDIA

### Media Lists and Sources (Including E-zine Lists)
www.baconsmedialists.com/
www.mediafinder.com
www.lifestylespub.com
www.infojump.com/
www.ezinesearch.com
http://ezine-universe.com/
www.list-city.com/ezines.htm
http://www.gebbieinc.com/
http://www.press1.net/
http://www.mediamap.com/
http://www.radiodirectory.com/

### Press Release Services
www.newsbureau.com/
http://www.ereleases.com/
http://www.cyberalert.com/

### Press Release Services (continued)
http://www.send2press.com/
www.onlinepressreleases.com/
www.gopressrelease.com/
www.urlwire.com/
www.prnewswire.com
www.businesswire.com
www.iwire.com
http://www.corporatenews.com/
www.ideaagent.com/

### Publication and Periodical Directories
www.newsdirectory.com/
www.publist.com/
usnewspapers.about.com/cs/papersall/
www.library.fullerton.edu/elecpubsdir.htm
www.altpress.org/direct.html
www.winwriters.com/resperio.htm
www.entrepreneurbooks.com/

## REFERENCES and SELF-HELP

### Experts, Forums, and Message Boards
www.exp.com/
www.refdesk.com/expert.html
http://www.askjeeves.com/
http://www.allexperts.com/
http://www.freeadvice.com/
http://askanexpert.com/
www.catalog.com/corner

### Online Tutorials and Self-Help Training
www.findtutorials.com/
www.e-learningcenter.com/
www.tutorials.com/

### *Online Tutorials and Self-Help Training (continued)*
www.worldwidelearn.com/
http://hansworse.freeyellow.com/
www.freeskills.com/
www.programmingtutorials.com/
www.webproforum.com/
www.adobe.com/products/tips/photoshop.html
http://www.emtech.net/tutorials_on_net.htm
http://blackboard.com/
http://www.virtualpromote.com/
www.learn2.com

### *University and Foundation Centers for Entrepreneurship*
www.babson.edu/entrep/
www.celcee.edu/
entrepreneurship.mit.edu/
www.nfte.com/
www.rhsmith.umd.edu/dingman/
www.slu.edu/eweb/
www.entrepreneurship.com/
www.entre-ed.org/
www.ncoe.org/
www.haas.berkeley.edu/lester/
www.gcase.org/
hsb.baylor.edu/entrepreneur/default.asp
www.nyie.org/
www.cob.fsu.edu/jmi/
www.uclamba.com/

## WEBSITES

### *Awards for Websites and Small Businesses*
websiteawards.xe.net/
www.webbyawards.com/
http://www.awardforum.com/

### Awards (continued)
http://www.awardsites.com/
http://smallbusinesssuccess.sba.gov/
www.hkyoungit.com/
www.ey.com/

### Email Autoresponders
http://www.autobots.net/
http://www.automagical.net/
http://www.biz-e-bot.com/
http://followingup.com/
http://freeautobot.com/
www.sendfree.com/
http://www.getresponse.com/
autoresponders.org/
www.autoresponders.com/
www.freeautoresponders.net/
followingup.com/

### Web Content and Content Management (Including Several Free Content Sites)
http://www.content-exchange.com/
http://www.buy-sell-econtent.com/
http://www.infooffice.com/
http://certificate.net/wwio/
http://ezinearticles.com/
http://subportal.iboost.com/
http://www.web-source.net/syndicator.htm
http://loska.com/free/
http://www.doctorebiz.com/
http://www.4freecontent.com/
www.contentbiz.com
www.internetcontent.net
www.brillscontent.com
www.content-wire.com
www.clickz.com

## Web Development

www.wdvl.com/
www.webreference.com/
www.webdeveloper.com/
www.devshed.com/
www.pageresource.com/
www.website-works.com
www.webmasterslibrary.com/
www.webdevelopersjournal.com/
http://webdevelopment.developersnetwork.com/

## Web Hosting

www.fortunecity.com/
www.webjump.com/
www.easyspace.com/
www.prohosting.com/
www.valueweb.net/
www.icom.com/
www.virtualave.net/
www.tophosts.com/
www.addr.com/

## Website Traffic Building

www.trafficbuilding.com/
www.virtual-stampede.com/
www.bizpromo.com/
www.click-traffic.com/
www.hyperhit.net/
www.trafficgeneration.com/